# Snapshots
## The Life of a Gringo in Mexico

# Snapshots
## The Life of a Gringo in Mexico

by
## Sam Grubb

This is a work of fiction. Names, characters, businesses, places, events and incidents are either the products of the author's imagination or used in a fictitious manner. Any resemblance to actual persons, living or dead, or actual events is purely coincidental.

# Contents

## *Dedication*

To my wife, the Princess who loves me very much and who thinks that this book is the dumbest thing I have ever done, so far.

## *Acknowledgements*

I would like to thank Kat Hammontre, who started and encouraged me on this path, Terry Van Arsdale who pushed me and Denny and Sandi Flannigan who kept me going, and Julie, without whom this book would not have been possible.

I would also like to thank all the little people, some of whom I've already forgotten.

# *Reviews*

I started writing about two years ago. There was no reason for it, it just seemed like I had to do it. At first there was no intention to share it with anyone. Then it evolved into sharing with my wife, then some family members, and finally friends and family. No one said much about them, which was just fine. Then one day Kat contacted me and said that she had heard about my stories and would like to post them on her website. At first I refused, not wanting to publicly expose myself, but she persisted, and I relented. What followed has shocked me! People actually wrote comments that were complimentary. After three months there has not been one negative remark from readers. It has completely stunned me that anyone would find them that interesting. Here are some of the reviews from those close to me:

"That's nice, but you could have done better." –**Your Mother**

"Where in the world do you come up with this stuff?" – **Your Wife**

"Who?"                           - **Henry Kissinger**

"Have you considered exorcism?"      - **Wendy**

"Are you on prescription drugs?"      - **Terry Van Arsdale**

"You need professional help."        - **Your Family**

With that kind of support and encouragement a person could become conceited and have a grossly exaggerated view of his talent. People actually come up to me in public and tell me what they think about my writing. This kind of fame is a heady thing. At least 6 or 7 people read the postings every week. There are visions of publishing a book that is translated into 14 languages and outsells the Bible. So far however, I haven't received a single penny for my artistic endeavors, but to us real artists, it's not about the money, it's about creating a masterpiece. OK so that is bullshit. It is about the money. I just hope that I don't have to die before I become famous.

## Mother's Funeral

Most of my stories start with a smattering of truth, but then tend to wander into the arena of embellishment and even fantasy. A rigorous attention to what really happened is notably lacking. This story has not even a hint of makeup. It's just as it really happened, because it already strains the bounds of credibility. I would like to add that I had the feeling of mother's presence there, and that she thought the whole thing was funny. So, here goes, the story of mom's funeral:

First a little background. Mom's health had been deteriorating for some time, and it came to the time that we all hoped her suffering would soon end. My sisters all live busy lives, and I have golf tournaments to play. There were also the logistical problems presented by family that lived all over the USA and in my case Mexico. We would have to book airline tickets for all these people. So, to make things more convenient, we chose a date for the funeral, based on our best guesses of when she would go. (I chose a date that would fit around a tournament in Tijuana.) So anyway, we started the planning process, buying tickets and arranging housing. Well, as we approached the date, mother still hadn't died. We were in a real quandary. Would she mind if we buried her anyway? Would anyone notice? Finally, just a couple of days before the funeral she did pass away. What a relief, both for her and for us.

The arrangements were simple. Twenty-five years ago when dad died, mom bought a double plot for both of their ashes. So all we had to do was tell the mortuary that no we didn't want the cherry wood casket to cremate her, the cardboard one would be just fine. Then we had to design a simple service. My sisters all tend to be literate, and knew just what they wanted. Just a simple graveside service with a few bible passages. One of them remembered that mom used to be a church secretary, and she and the minister were good friends. So they tracked him down and asked him to do the service. He said that although he was retired, he would be honored to do that for Doris. We agreed to meet about an hour before the service to put together the program. We also hired a catering service to feed everyone at home afterwards. OK, now we're ready. As simple as it was, if you've ever been through the process, you know that by now we're worn out with trips to the airport to pick up family, housing them, feeding them, and taking care of details. So finally the day of the funeral arrived, and that's when things started going crazy.

The minister arrived about 45 minutes before the service. He was on oxygen, in a wheelchair, and had Alzheimer's. We showed him what we wanted, and it was very obvious that nobody was home. We agreed that the oldest sister would sit next to him and guide him through the service. That would work. Now we have about 25 minutes until kickoff, and people are starting to arrive. The funeral director came in and here is a synopsis of his speech:

"I want you to understand that it's not my fault. We only control what happens here in the office, and what happens out there is the maintenance department. We have no responsibility for what they do. So there is nothing we can do to solve this problem, because it's not our department." This continued for several minutes, until I interrupted him and asked him what the hell he was talking about. He finally 'fessed up and told us there was no spot for mom's ashes. Picture this: Three sisters on the verge of tears. They wanted closure. I wanted to kill that fat bastard. So we demanded that he bring in the head of the maintenance dept. I asked him if he could put mom's ashes in with dad. He said, "Yes." Can you do it in 15 minutes? He said, "Yes". I said, "Do it." Problem solved. Now all we had to do is go to the gravesite, have the service, host a party and we're done.

So we hauled the minister out to the gravesite, wheeled him up on the grass, and luckily it was a nice Northwest spring day. No rain. So we began the service. The minister started his homily. It was a story about a little girl who wanted a puppy, so her father bought her one. Then she wanted a doghouse for the puppy, so father built her one. But, the puppy wouldn't go into it and she was very disappointed in her father. She decided that just maybe, if she

6

went in it, the puppy would follow her. Sure enough, it worked. That's the end of the homily. At this point my little sister cracked and said, "Does this mean that mother is in the doghouse?" We ignored her. So now my big sister is guiding him through the ceremony, and things were going smoothly, that is until about halfway through the service my aunt, mother's sister fell down and had a stroke. I called 911 and in a matter of minutes we had a fire truck, and aid car, and a whole bunch of medics with armloads of equipment storming the site. Everyone was gathered around her watching this drama unfold, and the preacher sat there smiling and continuing the service. We finally shut him up, got my aunt hauled to the hospital, and then resumed the service. Finally, we made it! The service was over, and we felt that in spite of the problems, it had been a good service.

So now we wheeled the minister off the grass onto the pavement to put him in the car. Someone else was carrying his large oxygen bottle for him. Just as we dropped the wheelchair off the curb, the young man dropped the bottle. It was attached to the preacher's head with a harness. His head snapped like a whiplash. I was sure that we'd just broken his neck. Luckily there must have been enough flexibility in the plastic hose that no serious damage was done.

Well it's over, and now we can relax. Well not quite. We had about 40 people show up at the house expecting to drink and eat. The drinking was just fine, but the catering service brought snacks instead of a meal. So now we have to rush to the store and buy food, and cook for those who weren't quick enough on the first round. And just to add the perfect finish to the day, by the time all this was handled, and I was really, really ready to unwind, all the gin was gone.

Mother sometimes had a wicked sense of humor. I still wonder how much of that she engineered, as a final shot as revenge for all the heartache we gave her growing up.

# Car Repairs

Took the Jeep in for a routine physical last week. You know, just the standard stuff. Blood test, Urinalysis, X ray etc. The mechanic changed its body fluids, and passed holy water over it. Here in San Felipe we do things differently than in the big city of Mexicali. Up there they have computer diagnosis, trained mechanics, and all the usual things to justify charging a young fortune to do whatever it is that they do to make cars run. In San Felipe a full set of tools consists of an old set of pliers, some wire, and a little bit of used duct tape. Occasionally you will see evidence of chickens being sacrificed to cure electrical problems. The mechanic here is a wonderful man. He's very resourceful, and has a gentle sense of humor. Over his shop is a big sign that says, "Broken Inglish spoken here". He can make anything run. The problem is that for so many years, these people have had to make do with no training or proper equipment that they have become experts at the temporary fix. This history is so deeply ingrained, that it doesn't occur to them to replace a broken part. A typical exchange when you pick up your car would be,

Customer: "Is my car ready?"

Mechanic: "Not quite. Maybe 5 more minutes." (Translation: I haven't started on it yet, but after lunch will look at it")

Customer: "OK, I'll wait." (Note: This customer has not lived in San Felipe very long. The correct answer is: "OK, I'll stop by tomorrow")

If the customer does wait, after 6 to 7 hours the narrative would look like:

Mechanic: "Everything's done. She's running fine."

Customer: Great. How much do I owe you?"

Mechanic: (After scratching his head and looking at the ground for a while) says

"un mil pesos"

Customer: OK thanks for your help"

Mechanic: "Oh, by the way your accelerator linkage was broken, so I ran this wire from the engine to the emergency brake. When you want to go, just pull on the brake handle, and to stop, just push while you gear down, because I had to unhook your brakes."

At this point there are several options:

1. Losing your temper, which is not really an option. He thought he was doing you a favor.

2. Starting a protracted negotiation to convince him to order a new linkage and install it when it arrives.

3. Drive the car to the States, and have it fixed.

Option three is probably the best. I tried option two once. After paying in advance for the part and a month of waiting for the part, the mechanic moved to Sinaloa with his sister-in-law. No one has seen him or the part in over a year.

Lest you think I'm throwing rocks at the local mechanics, let me assure you that this is typical of all the trades. Anything that works properly is viewed with some suspicion here. We have friends who had a house built, and it had one electrical breaker for the entire house. They couldn't use both the kitchen lights and the microwave at the same time, let alone have anything else in the house on. The electrician didn't understand why you would want to. It's all part of the charm of living an unhurried, patient life. Down here you learn not to over react. No one is foaming at the mouth or threatening to sue somebody. We just learn how to make do, just like the natives do. By the way, if you want them to change oil, you need to bring oil with you. They don't buy oil here.

## *Misc.*

Good morning everyone. Life has been pretty full lately, and thought I would explain how I've been justifying my existence. The woman that we discussed merger with, and subsequently decided against, has gone to one of our partners and made him a ridiculous offer for his stock. He accepted. The basis for her doing that was that she had looked at our financial statements earlier, and thought they were in dollars, not pesos. So the thought we were making 10 times as much as we are. So we are upset that this shark may be our partner, and she's upset, accusing us of misleading her. It's like a girl I once knew. From a distance she was fine. Up close she was ugly.

A few weeks ago I ran into a friend downtown who has a coffee shop. He told me that he had lost his lease. I told him that maybe we could build him a coffee shop on the corner of our property at the storage company. He said, "Great." I said I would check on building codes, and costs and let him know in a week or so. On Monday I stopped by his store to have coffee, and there was a notice on the window that said, "We are moving to San Felipe Storage Co. on Dec. 1. Thank you Sam for your help." Hmmm. So we haven't really negotiated the lease yet, I still don't have a handle on all the construction costs, but we are doing the site work, and pouring the concrete slab next week. In the meantime he has set up a coffee shop in our office to keep the business running while we build. The only thing that is definite about this deal is that I get free coffee. Well, that and the fact that we're spending a bunch of money on a new building. Oddly, the thing that made this possible is a surveyor error, that was just discovered a month ago. We thought that the storage building was on the property line, but when we finally received title to the property we had about 70 feet in front and 45 feet on the side.

Diane is up in Holtville visiting her daughter, Berkeley this week. I'll bet there is some shopping going on too. (shudder). So, it's a wild bachelor week here in San Felipe. Monday night I had a dozen people over for dinner. Had a great time. No one went home until 9:00 PM. The next morning the kitchen was a mess. Empty beer cans, liquor bottles, dirty dishes - you can picture the scene. The thing that had me laughing out loud was that instead of a bra hanging from the doorknob, there was my apron. It's a pathetic commentary on getting old.

So, golf continues to be mediocre (playing like an amateur), the sunrises continue to be spectacular, and every day is a gift.

## On Being a Husband

I keep being reminded that being a good husband is a baffling experience. We won't try to relive the incident a few weeks ago when I fell asleep during cocktails with guests. I know that was perhaps a little rude,. but you would have to know those guests to completely understand. I was reminded again today just how difficult husbanding really is.

Yesterday my wife mentioned that she had a hair appointment, so when I got home I said, "Your hair looks good."

She said, " My appointment was rescheduled for tomorrow."

So today after golf I didn't say anything. Wrong again! She actually had the hair thing today. Now she is upset because I didn't notice her new hair color. How is a man supposed to know when hair is different? I mean if she had a boob job, it would be callous not to notice, but how can you tell if hair is different? Its like minor changes around the house. New towels, bedspreads, drapes, a new couch or new paint in the living room (although the smell of paint may be a tip off here) are things that most of us men won't notice. Questions like, "What are you going to wear to the party tomorrow?, What should I wear?, What is everyone else wearing?, Do these colors go together?, will stump any man. I can't imagine even thinking about what to wear until 5 minutes before we leave. Statements like, "Let's just spend the evening talking and sharing our feelings, or discussing the state of the marriage of everyone we know," are the major cause of panic attacks in men. For men relationships are pretty straightforward. Are you getting any or not? There's not much else to talk about, except the details.

In all fairness, I get a blank stare when we discuss curl patterns, slant routes, or post patterns vs. a 3-4 defense. She has no opinion whether to lay up or go for the green on the 11th hole. I must say however, that these are important and complex issues that can challenge the intellect. They can also have a serious impact on the family income. I made $2 by laying up on 11 today, but lost money betting on the Chargers in the playoffs last year.

After golf today the boys were in the bar discussing the complexities of living with women. We had proposed solutions ranging from homicide to suicide, with several more moderate positions in between. We noticed that the extremists hadn't actually played golf. They'd been in the bar all day punishing their livers. There was a common theme to all of the opinions. The solution boiled down to spending a life of humility and penitence, praying for forgiveness. It sounds just like being a monk. The tricky part is to know just when we've done something requiring absolution. Major mistakes aren't too hard to spot. Forgetting things like anniversaries (first date, first kiss, first fight, wedding etc.), birthdays, Christmas, forgetting to pick up milk on the way home, forgetting to tell her you've invited 20 people for dinner. Those are mortal sins. It's the venal sins that we've been discussing that can be confusing. Well, I love her dearly and on the whole, she's worth it all.

## *On Retiring*

While your job schedules begin to unravel

I'll be deciding where next to travel

When all of your bids come in second or thirds

I'll be out trying to identify birds.

When you're being frustrated by recalcitrant subs

I'll be on golf courses using my clubs

When you're eaten alive by the paperwork trap

I'll be at home, taking a nap.

When you're so frustrated you can't even see

I'll be at relaxing and watching TV

But my life won't be perfect; I'll sometimes be blue

Cause I'll miss two things, that's payday and you.

## Shortest Day of The Year

I'll have to write fast, because this is the shortest day of the year. Tomorrow will be 4 seconds longer than today, and the sun will be starting its journey North for the summer. The sun will peek over the horizon in about 10 minutes at 6:30 and disappear at about 5:00 tonight. It seems odd that the coldest month is January, when the days are already lengthening. It takes until mid-February for the cold to fade away, and the warmth of spring to return to our village. Until then it's long pants and sweatshirts. I even wear socks. The Mexicans look like little teddy bears all bundled up. They are wearing down coats and hooded sweatshirts in 50 to 60 degree weather. We're all just glad we're not up north in a blizzard, although it's hard to feel like Christmas without really cold weather. We will probably play golf on Christmas day.

Christmas Eve I have been hired to play Christmas carols on the piano for a party. The hosts have a piano, but don't know how to play it. I went over and tried it the other day. It was awful. Hadn't been tuned in the last century, so they had it tuned last week. Everyone please pray that I remember how to play. I do really miss having a piano at home. My wages for this gig are to be taken out in drinks and food. That will be expensive for them.

Diane is struggling through her annual cold. She is just miserable. Monday I took her out into the desert to the home of a healer. She waved a feather over her body, made strange noises, and took all of the bad energy and threw it into the center of the earth. Diane was so sore that night that she couldn't move. She is going back Monday to do it again. Hmmm. After the treatment we went to the health food store for more magic potions. Hmmm. The lady who owns the health food store is a fascinating person. If someone publishes an article on the health benefits of something, she buys into it. Last summer she had Diane taking clay, adding water and drinking the mud. Two farmers from the Midwest had published a little book on the benefits of a special type of clay. The book told how wonderful it was for your health, without ever saying what it did. It turns out that this special clay could be found on the farmer's property. Pretty clever huh? Can't grow anything in that dirt, so sell it and make a young fortune. I swear that if someone were to write an article on the benefits of eating ground rabbit droppings, she would promote and sell it.

Well, I'd like to say Merry Christmas to those of you who are not offended by the religious undertones of the phrase. I do so with no intent to offend those of other religious or agnostic or atheist persuasions. There is also no intent to offend those of alternative lifestyle or sexual orientation. I have no intent of infringing on the rights of others to view it as a strictly commercial venture to be exploited for profit. To be truthful, I really don't care what you think about the holiday. Just quit your bitching and enjoy yourself.

## Snapshots

The sunrise this morning was a stunner! There was a tiny layer of clouds just a little above the horizon running parallel to the horizon. They left a little room for the sun to take a look around before hiding behind them. There were still a few stars that hadn't closed their eyes and gone to bed, and the clouds were doing a light show that went from pale pastels to bright oranges and reds. The mountains behind town turned a bright pink. They look like they're embarrassed at being caught naked after doing whatever it is that mountains do all night. It was a great show, enhanced by good coffee and a totally quiet town. Mornings here are spectacular.

We have a new four-lane highway, leaving town now, complete with a center dividing strip, painted stripes, and road signs for safety. Last week someone crashed into the "Fasten your seatbelt for safety" sign. As you approach one of the intersections there are white arrows on the pavement so drivers won't become confused. Some of the arrows point the wrong way.

A dear friend of ours has had a problem with burglary lately. She tried staying awake all night, but realized that wouldn't work very well long term. She kept falling asleep. So, she decided that a watch-dog would be the perfect answer. She is not familiar with the ways of animals, not counting a few of her old boyfriends. Anyway, she called the animal rescue shelter and they told her they had a one-year-old housebroken dog that would be perfect. No one knows exactly what happened, but instead of that dog, she came home with a dog named Bodacious. He's at least ten years old. You don't need a leash to walk him. He needs either a walker or a stretcher. He has three teeth and bad breath. He will occasionally bark at other dogs, but never at humans. He spends a lot of time sticking his head in a bush and rubbing it on the branches. Our friend called yesterday and asked how you can tell if a dog has ticks in his ears. We told her to lift the ear and look. She said, "What do they look like?" We described a tick. She said, "Ick, can't I just ask the vet?" We told her, "Yep" and gave her directions to the vet's office. Then she asked if she had to take the dog with her. It's probably a good idea, if you want the vet to look for ticks.

Last Saturday there was a poker run out in the desert. I think there is a law here that you are required to own a dune buggy, and a poker run is the perfect opportunity to show it off, and talk about suspension systems, fuel injection and all that mystical stuff that cars do. Incidentally, the drivers who talk the most about all their custom design high tech riggings are the ones who most often break down out in the middle of nowhere. The run is about a 60-mile circle out and back with checkpoints. Over a 1,000 people showed up for the run, but the beer truck didn't. This made the original Mexican Revolution pale by comparison. Dune buggies require more beer per mile than gasoline. I understand that. No one in their right mind would get into one of those things sober.

So we continue to dine elegantly at the banquet of life here, unfettered by any sense of reality.

# *Traffic Safety*

I'm sure most of you have seen TV footage of the Baja 1000 off road race. They always show pictures of cars racing through the desert or mountains at high rates of speed, bouncing off of rocks, throwing up big clouds of dust and generally doing heroic and stupid stuff. Actually those pictures are often not of the race, but normal driving practice in Mexico. Passing on the shoulder, passing into the teeth of an oncoming car, or just running over someone are accepted practice. The big difference is that here it is done with no malice. The people being run off the road don't seem to mind. I have never seen a case of road rage. Only once in 5 years have I seen someone extend the middle finger salute, and that was a tourist. It's easy to change lanes here without gunfire.

A recent incident is a good example. There was a traffic jam on the highway leading out of town. A traffic jam is 6 cars in a row, traveling at less than 50 miles an hour. The reason for the slowdown was a small Ford pickup with a horse in the back. The horse's eyes were wide, he had a foot in each corner of the bed, and if he could have reached it, he would have had the rearview mirror in his teeth. The road has no shoulders and just enough potholes to keep you alert. Potholes here have been known to swallow Volkswagens. But, I digress. Contrary to the popular stereotype of Mexicans of being laid back, when they get behind the wheel their juices start to flow. Once again, I digress. Anyway, back to the story, one of the cars in the line, a little Ford Focus, left the road, headed into the desert and passed the line. He was airborne most of that time. His passenger looked like a Keene picture, really, really big eyes. He then headed back onto the highway, getting an impressive amount of air as he jumped the drop-off of the pavement. Extraneous parts were falling off during this maneuver. The rear bumper ended up on the highway, causing cars to duck, swerve, and take to the desert themselves. The horse managed to stay in the truck, though he did relieve himself. Now in some areas of the world this would be an incident. Here, traffic just continued to flow without missing a beat.

It has become even more fun lately. They are widening the road out of town to 4 lanes. This means all the usual traffic diversions while they tear up the old and build the new. The construction standards are different here too. They don't waste a lot of money on barricades or detour markers. For the drivers it's an ideal opportunity for creative expression. When you have no idea where your lane is, or what the oncoming lane is supposed to be, it's every man for himself. The construction crews are pretty much on their own. Cars, not workers have the right-of-way. You have to admire their agility and athletic ability. I guess the slow ones just don't make it in that business. Every once in a while they do have a flagger. They are all trained the same way. They wave the flag just like they are swatting flies. You have no idea whether that means stop, go, or duck. After dark it's even more fun. You can be charging along, and suddenly the pavement ends. You bounce around, hit a few rocks, do your best to keep the shiny side up, and just keep on truckin'. The new highway will have a nice row of palm trees down the middle, but still no shoulders. People will still have to change tires, add gas or water, rebuild the engine or replace the transmission in the right lane. They are a brave and wonderful people.

## *Winter*

Well, winter came to San Felipe yesterday with a frontal assault on our little town. A fierce north wind came roaring down the street, strong enough to carry away little children and pets, like a scene from Mary Poppins. The shrimp trawlers were all huddled in the little cove in front of our house. They were hunkered down all day, trying to keep from being blown off the water. The blowing sand and dust assaulted the walls to our courtyard. They scaled the ramparts, and made mud pies in our swimming pool. The wind carried cold air from the mountains with it. The residents and the Thanksgiving tourists went to ground, much to the delight of local tavern keepers. So now we change from shorts to long pants, sweatshirts, and rummage around in our closets for bathrobes and furry slippers.

Now that Mother Nature has put us on notice, she gave us a break today. It's just beautiful outside. No wind. 60 degrees at dawn. The sunrise designed to make postcards for the tourist bureau. It's a day to savor, because we know that the next two months will be windy and chilly. It can be hard work, living in a third world country.

I've just been beginning to really notice the expatriate community here. I've been delighted and fascinated with the Mexican population. Their gentle, friendly ways just hold you in their embrace and make you forget the gringo lifestyle. There is a fairly large USA and Canadian population down here too. It makes sense that they are all a little different. Anyone who intentionally leaves their homeland to live in another country has to have something different in their makeup. The relationships among them are quite different. No one talks about what they did "Up North", or "On the other side". Down here you're known by what you do for fun. Dune buggies in the desert, fishing, building a solar house, golf, drinking, or in some cases, no explanation at all. There is an openness in the relationships, but carefully defined boundaries that do not include a lot of talk about where your money comes from. Maybe describing one of them will help.

There's the 90-day wonder. No one knows his name. He's a tall handsome man about 45 years old. His name came from the fact that his marriages last about 90 days. In his defense I must admit that he has been married to the same woman several of those times. No one knows where his money comes from, but it doesn't matter. He's a nice guy and fun to be around.

A typical night out for special occasions here would start with dinner at the Langosta Roja. It's nice with well-trained waiters, good ambience, good food, and Mexican guitar players to add an authentic touch to the dinner. After dinner it is required that you walk down the block to Al's Backstreet Bar. It has low ceilings, is painted black, bras and panties nailed to the ceiling. There's a douche bag hanging behind the bar with "Diane" lettered on it. (yep, its hers). There are two pool tables, a few high, narrow tables with hard wood stools. Its loud, filled with smoke. In short, seedy beyond belief. Out back is a patio with a corrugated roof over part of it. They serve food there, mostly for bachelors who don't know how to cook for themselves. Food poisoning obviates the need for a desert menu. The wine list features easy open screw top bottles. For some strange reason the place is always packed with gringos. The rich and famous mingle with the drunk and broke here. Social class doesn't matter here. Oddly, there's never any fights or even unpleasantness here. It's our version of going to the country club. Well, maybe not quite, but close enough.

Remember that friendship is like peeing your pants. Everyone can see it, but only you can experience the warmth.

## Elk Hunting

Some time ago my buddy, Earl, talked me into going elk hunting with him. I knew better, but sometimes we all make bad decisions in the name of male bonding. Just so you know, all the elk are safe, and they probably enjoyed watching those crazy people freezing their butts off for no good reason.

To start at the beginning, Chinook Pass was closed, so I left Wednesday night and drove around through Ellensberg and Yakima and back into the eastside of the mountains to Whistling Jack's Resort. Resort is a euphemism for some shabby rooms and a bar. The motel office was closed so I thought I would have to sleep in the car. I heard music from the bar, and decided to check it out before turning in. What a sight! There were no women in the bar, just hunters. They were all huge, ugly, dirty, mean looking men, all drinking straight shots, and emitting palpable scents of testosterone. I haven't seen anything like that since I was a kid growing up in Eastern Oregon. These guys were probably all lawyers and doctors, and CPA's but let them grow a beard, carry a gun, and have a few drinks, and they revert to primitive hunters. Actually, as my eyes adjusted to the light, they weren't as big and mean as they looked. They were just fat.

Anyway, I sat at the bar and ordered my usual tonic, and said to the bartender, "Looks like the motel is all full up, huh?

He said, "Nope, ya want a room?"

I said, "Yep.

He said, "You want the riverside suite, with a hot tub?"

I said, "Nope, just a place to sleep."

He said, "OK" and signed me in.

If you are in a generous mood, you could call the room quaint. No TV, no phone, no nothing. Well, there was a bed.

The sign out front said, "Breakfast 6AM," So I set the alarm and went to sleep, already missing my wife and the comforts of home.

I was up long before dawn cracked, ready for a mountain breakfast before I headed into the hills. Nothing was open. After a few minutes of wandering, I figured out that the clock in my room was still on daylight savings time, and it was only 5 AM. So I just hung out in my new insulated boots, 3 layers of long underwear, army surplus wool pants, borrowed red wool shirt, and Australian cowboy hat, pumping on my male hormones. An hour later there was still no sign of life in the restaurant, so I went to the convenience store, and the lady there told me that they didn't do much breakfast business since they opened the bar a night, so they quit opening. She did have a microwave version of the egg McMuffin. Already I'm roughing it, and not even into the woods yet.

Still not listening to the voice in the back of my head screaming, "Don't do this!" I drove into the mountains to the packer's cabin. He wasn't much for conversation. He was a genuine, old time cowboy. He was tall, skinny, bowlegged and complete with leather chaps, about 70 years old, and tougher than nails. He saddled the horses and leaped onto one. I led mine over to a stump, and stood on it while I tried to lift my leg high enough to reach the stirrup. I flopped onto the horse, and felt like I was trying to straddle a kitchen table, but there wasn't time to adjust, because the packer was disappearing up a cliff with his horse. I clung to the horse up the mountain, across rivers, over dead trees, along trails six inches wide, hanging over sheer drop-offs, higher than the eye could see for over two hours. When we arrived at camp, I was seriously concerned that I may be permanently crippled. It would not have been macho to admit to any pain, but at that point I would have killed for some Advil and a hot tub. After the howdys were said, and everyone had a cup of coffee, the packer left. I felt like a kid on the first day of school. I didn't want to stay there. I wanted to go home, and the sight of the horses disappearing down the mountain was real depressing.

Let me describe the camp. It was so high in the mountains that it was above the tree line. What I saw was rocks and snow up to our butts. It was about noon, about 20 degrees, and Earl was excited that it had warmed up so much. It was so high and so cold that it hurt to breathe. The packer was going to come back in four days to pick us up, that is, if it didn't snow so much that he couldn't get back in. So here I was, the owner of a nice home in town with central heat and a hot tub, stuck for an indeterminate time in this canvas tent. There was a stove in the tent, that if fired full tilt could take a little of the chill off. The problem was that the stove leaked, so that the tent was always filled with smoke. We had a choice, suffocate or freeze. Just outside the tent was a propane stove that we used to cook grease. When you're male bonding the menu is bacon, sausage, fatty meats, all fried in the grease left from the last meal. In all fairness I must admit that I had a 6 pack of diet coke to wash it down with. I tried to eat and drink as little as possible for those 4 days because relieving yourself required a dangerous, painful process of exposing part of your body to the weather. The pioneers must have had sex only in the summers, although mosquitoes make that risky too.

Sleeping was the best part of the trip. We had down sleeping bags and air mattresses, which were quite warm. The more time I slept, the less time there was to sit around camp and wait for horses to get me out of there. Finally, the golden moment did arrive. After four days to 10 to 20 degree weather, interrupted by a brief torrential rain, that then froze and turned the mountain into a sheet of ice, the packer returned!!! He also brought 6 mules to haul out our stuff. We finally got it all loaded up and headed down the mountain. One of the mules kept laying down, and I wanted to just leave the son of a bitch there, but the packer insisted that it should come with us. I would have gladly paid for the mule and all of his gear, just to get out of there. We finally did make it to the bottom, loaded all the gear into the truck, and headed for home. That's when the diarrhea set in.

For two days I sat on the pot and reflected on why in the world anyone would want to go hunting when you can just go to Larry's market and buy food that is much better than anything that's up in those godforsaken mountains.

# Murray The Cigar Man

He wasn't Murray Goldberg, or Murray the husband, or Murray the clothier. He was Murray the cigar man. That brings to mind a story about a bridge builder, but we'll save that for another time. Last night we had a memorial dinner for him to celebrate his life. Out of our love and respect for him, we almost killed ourselves too. It turned into an evening that would have made him proud. Murray was the most reliable source of gossip in San Felipe. Anything of any significance, and some things of no value was discussed at his cigar shop where he held court. If Murray liked you, you could not have a better friend. If he didn't he was hilarious in putting you down. He had more friends than anyone I have known. There were about 30 people at the dinner, and everyone there talked about what a good friend he was. We shared memories of him, and pictures of his last lap dance over cocktails, wine, after dinner drinks and a few nightcaps.

As if this wasn't enough we had to uphold the tradition of going to Al's for another drink. For those of you who have lived your lives in monasteries or nunneries, Al's is a little bar that features black walls, underwear on the ceiling and smoke so thick you can almost cut it with a knife. It's San Felipe's version of a country club. The juke box plays rock and roll at a volume that discourages serious conversation. It's mostly limited to, "Do you want another drink?" or the demand from a seriously drunk patron, "Dance with me." Anyway, this is the part where fate intervened, and made it the perfect memorial for Murray.

Sitting next to me was a young woman who introduced herself. She had a spectacular chest, a sleeveless blouse, and no bra. She also happened to be very outgoing. She gave the command, "Dance with me." I quivered. Being the married man that I am, and totally devoted to my wife (Diane – this part is for you) I grabbed Dan and pushed him in front of her. I have never seen a dog drool quite like Dan did. She had moves that defied both the laws of physics and of decency. (That's what others told me later. I, of course, didn't look.) The evening was progressing nicely as the volume increased, and what little conversation there was became only semi coherent. As the boys got better acquainted with her, they learned that she owned a brothel. Her popularity rating went through the roof with this revelation. Dan finally had to sit down and take some heart medication. We came within inches of having it be a memorial dinner for two guys in one night.

I hate it when someone tells only part of a story and leaves you in suspense, but I am going to have to commit that sin now. The rest of the evening is either too hazy to recount, or covered by Federal Confidentiality laws. It was the perfect evening for a good friend, who we won't miss because he's still a part of us.

# *Baja Sunrise*

It starts with just a hint of orange on the horizon. Everything is in place for the ceremony. There is a low fog bank on the mainland horizon topped by a thicker band of clouds that are shaped like the silhouette of a mountain range. On the far end is a vertical cloud imitating a volcano. Above that layer are some horizontal streaks that have been painted by a delicate cosmic brush, then a few dabs above that to clean the brush. As the oranges change from pastel to vivid they start to spread along the horizon until they stretch from end to end. Pastels on the extremes, vivid in the center. The clouds start to change from black to grey to white. This morning the sea is flat. Its slack tide so there is no sound from the surf, just a little gentle lapping. It's like a gentle snoring, only nicer than when we do it. The colors of the sunrise start to reflect on the water. As the ceremony unfolds the colors become brighter and more complex. Words can't convey the complexities of the shading and the gradually increasing intensity. The world is completely still, breathlessly waiting for the performance to unfold. The only sound in this symphony is the chirping of crickets in their mating call. (I wonder if hiding behind a rock and chirping would work for me?) As the sun approaches the horizon the colors lighten in a chorus of praise. Finally the big moment and the sun peeks through the clouds, and everything fades to grays, whites and clear. The clouds have done their job, and they start to fade until tomorrow morning. As the ceremony concludes, the world starts to awaken. Crews go to work, families start breakfast, and some of us just drink a second cup of coffee. The intricacy and beauty of the sunrise ceremony leaves me with a sense of awe and an appreciation for the delicacy of our world and our lives.

By mid morning all the clouds will be gone and the sun will be hammering us with its summer intensity. The heat will melt the weak, and drive the children into the water to swim. The ocean is almost too warm in August, but still refreshing. The heat also inspired me to invent Mexican haiku. Here is the first poem written in this form:

## *Entertaining Friends*

Yesterday was an interesting day. Some of the boys needed help to fill out a foursome to play golf. I didn't want to play, but what can you do? When a friend needs help, you step up to the plate, or actually in this case, the tee. Wives don't often understand all of this. It's like the "Call of the Wild". When a buddy calls and says, "Can you play today?" family obligations, prior commitments, and global warming fade from consciousness. So we started playing about 10:00AM. It was a perfect day for golf. About 90 degrees with a little breeze. Our focus was entirely on the game for the first couple of hours. About half way through the match, out of nowhere, appeared the beverage cart. Now our course doesn't have many players on it, so the poor girl driving the cart doesn't make much money. Purely out of sympathy we bought some beer from her. She leaned over and smiled at us when we paid. It made it all worth while. Dave, who has been married for 40 years seriously considered running away from home. We had to remind him that he was $2.00 up, and had a moral obligation to give us a chance to get even. It is so satisfying to be able to save a marriage. However, the intensity of the game started to slip a little at that point.

There is a couple whose condo is on the 16th tee. We usually stop and have a beer with them. They have left for 6 weeks to visit family so we had encouraged them (blackmail is such an ugly word) to buy a refrigerator, put it on their deck, and fill it with beer. We are honor bound to take advantage of their thoughtfulness. The pace of play slowed a little at that point, but we persevered and finished the game, which is somewhat of a misnomer, because its not a game. It's serious business. When we finished, some money changed hands. It's against the law in Baja to win money and not buy a drink for the losers. So we went to the bar. If you have a drink after golf you are required to relive the round, discuss all the good and bad shots, and compare our shotmaking to that of Tiger Woods. By this time we are convinced that we could probably beat him.

So no problem, right? Well, not quite. Diane had invited friends over that afternoon for a swim and dinner. I was a little late arriving home, but was fully prepared to be a gracious and charming husband. The guests were already there, and I noticed that the temperature dropped significantly when I walked in. The foolproof strategy in this situation is to refill people's drinks, and keep quiet and smile and nod. I did that in spectacular fashion. When it came to the nod part, I nodded off and started snoring. The siesta is an integral part of Baja life, for some of us, approaching a spiritual ritual. For others it's viewed a little differently. Diane is one who views it differently. Our friends saw it as charming. Well, maybe not charming, but at least not too offensive. Diane mentioned something about revenge. I am a brave man, but her idea of revenge is frightening. She is very creative, and wicked. (In a loving way, of course) I have this awful feeling that this will be one of those things that lasts for the rest of my life. There was a minor incident 15 years ago, when she was unhappy with me. In an attempt to cheer her up I told her that she'd get over it. That still comes up regularly. A little slip, like falling asleep in the middle of entertaining guests could last a lifetime. My only hope is to get out to the golf course before she wakes up, and maybe she'll cool off by the time I get home tonight. Or maybe I should stay home and be attentive all day, or maybe having a heart attack would divert her attention for a little while. Well, we'll see what happens today. One thing I do know for sure, is that any advise from the boys at the golf course will be totally misguided, and foolish to follow.

# *January*

More Americans die in January than any other month. Why? Who knows, but we can speculate. January is a dark month. It follows the excitement of the holiday season, and most importantly, there is nothing funny about January. It doesn't offer the hope that February and March do. It is cold and foreboding and doesn't promise any relief from its bleak days. The parties are over, and it is now time to get serious. It's time to go to work.

As individuals we often reflect the seasons. People are more serious in January and it kills them. The "dark night of the soul" occurs when January presses down on us with its heavy weight of darkness. So how can we survive this test of the human spirit? We can create our own seasons. We, like the flowers, flourish with light and warmth, and we can create that world in our minds. We can picture ourselves laughing, running naked through the woods. We can visualize the warmth of a sunny beach, and we can enjoy the comfort of friends.

Regardless of what visions restore us, there is a common element to all of them. It's laughter. Picture your face when you feel happy, joyous or just relaxed. Do you see a smile? If not you're in trouble, you're a real boring person who wears pocket protectors for your pens and pencils, and you definitely have bad breath. People who don't laugh, or at least smile, are just the ones who are most susceptible to the January blues. They also have a downer effect on others, and often have a history of leprosy in their families. OK so maybe I'm exaggerating just a little bit. The point is that you can be popular, even if you're ugly and don't have white teeth or fragrant armpits. All you have to do is smile. We all know people who light up a room when they smile. Those are smiles that come from the core of your being. Laughter is a gift that you can give to others, and it's easily returned. It is the light of happiness that defeats January's oppressiveness. It will improve your sex life too. Well, maybe not, but what do you have to lose?

So let's all give the cosmic finger to January's depression. Let's turn on the light and warmth that's inside and reaffirm our faith that spring is indeed germinating deep down inside of us and in the rest of the world too.

# *Language*

Just spent last weekend in Cabo looking at a project, and getting the construction process started. That meant a 6-hour drive to San Diego to catch a plane back into Mexico. The flight was a madhouse, with all the usual frustrations heaped on hapless travelers. By the luck of the draw, I ended up seated next to a woman with a baby. Sure 'nuff, as soon as the plane took off the baby started crying. The woman immediately started breast-feeding the baby. She looked at me and apologized, saying that the Dr. said that it would equalize the pressure in his ears. And all these years I've been chewing gum.

You may wonder what us men think about when spending hours in cars, airports, airplanes and motels. Well, let me tell you what occurred to me during this trip. I started by thinking about the alphabet. When you are flopping about between two languages, English and Spanish, these things can be confounding. For example, what value does the letter "H" have? It is a wide letter, so it takes up a lot of space, and for the most part its silent. If we just ignored it, no serious damage would be done to the language. (My friend Hal objects to this line of thought.) Then there's the letter "E". It is ok when it's in the middle of a word, but put it at the end, and it becomes totally unreliable. You can't tell whether it messes with the pronunciation of the rest of the word, is pronounced itself, or is just hanging out there at the end. It looks to me like it wouldn't take too much effort to reduce the alphabet and make both spelling and pronunciation much easier than the current system.

OK, it took a couple of hours to figure that out. That, of course, led to musings on the bigger issue of language. Just look at Hawaiian. It has diarrhea of the vowels big-time. Some of their words are longer than a rope. It makes your mouth tired just thinking about trying to wrap your tongue around all those letters. Can you just imagine listening to a speech on hemorrhoids and open heart surgery in that language? It would take half the day just to introduce the speaker. On the other hand, the spoken word can be very effective. The last time I went to church the sermon acquainted me to two concepts that had previously eluded me. I now understand eternity. That's how long the sermon lasted. Heaven and hell now make sense too. Hell is like sitting in a pew that is harder than a whore's heart, in a stuffy room, listening to a speech that never ends. The only thing that made it bearable was thinking about going to heaven with that girl in the little sundress, two pews over and to the left. Of course the obvious solution would be not to even be there, but if you're underage you're pretty much at the mercy of your parents.

Now if the sermon had been in Chinese, it would have been much more effective. Their language is based on pictographic representations. The preacher could have just shown us some flashcards with pictures on them. In minutes the sermon would be over and we wouldn't have had a roomful of sore butts and stiff muscles.

So now I'm back in San Felipe, and won't have to think again for a while. That is a great relief to many people.

## Trip to Ensenada

Monday Paco and Robin invited us to go to Ensenada to a symphony concert at one of the vineyards over there. It's a 4-hour drive starting through the desert here and going over the mountains to the Pacific ocean side of the Baja. It's much like the Northwest there. Cool, often cloudy and a nice break from the heat here. The trip is breathtaking. There is actually occasional rain in the mountains, so the plants are GREEN. The Ocotillo cactus was covered with green leaves, the barrel cactus was twice the size of ours, and there were all kinds of other unnamed plants, all green. (They're unnamed due to my ignorance of botany.) It's a winding highway clinging to the edge of cliffs and numerous carcasses of trucks and cars who missed a turn. Paco loves to drive, so we had the luxury of just sightseeing.

We met some Mexican friends who took us to lunch at a fabulous restaurant hanging over the water. Just a few feet below our table the ocean was swirling around some boulders. It was spectacular. So was the food.. We checked into a motel, had a siesta and headed for the concert. This was an outdoor concert under the stars, on grass. First time I've seen grass in about a year. It was reserved tables with wine and cheese to nibble during the show. The orchestra was about 30 musicians who played Sebelius and Beethoven, and did a wonderful job, marred only by the conductor regularly looking back at the sound man and glaring. They had a pianist who studied in Italy, and he was amazing. After intermission they switched to opera. They had a soprano, mezzo-soprano and a tenor. They were awesome! It just carried you away. It was halfway through this program that the lighting tech. turned the spotlight on the singers. After two years in the desert with no nice restaurants, and no good music, it was a magical evening. At the end of the program the audience started chanting "Mas, mas," Español for "more". Of course they started an encore. Well, the vineyard, as a special surprise treat, planned a big fireworks show. They didn't explain the concept of encores to the pyrotecnicians. (classical music hardly exists here). You can see this coming, can't you? Yep. Just as they started the encore, the fireworks began. Neither one gave an inch. The singers were belting it out trying to cover the fireworks, and the fireworks guys were on a roll. The audience was on its feet, listening to the music, watching the fireworks and cheering. I was laughing so hard, I almost wet my pants. The rest of the trip was sooo relaxing. A good night's sleep, a gourmet breakfast at a fine French restaurant, and a leisurely trip home, back to the heat and sunshine. Life is good.

# *Rain*

Oh Boy! We awoke this morning as daylight was sliding into town to a steel grey sky. By about 6:30 it had started to rain. Nothing hard, just a pleasant drizzle. What a treat! After two years of no measurable rain, it's like a gift. I can just picture all the desert plants smiling, their faces turned skyward, their tongues out to feel the raindrops. As the day has progressed the rain continued, coming down a little harder all the time. By mid-morning the major intersections in town were flooded. The ground here is harder than a whore's heart, and totally impervious to penetration. (Unlike to the above mentioned woman) It doesn't take much rain to create floods, and general inconvenience for humans here in San Felipe. It would be a great day for a photographer. Rows of Mexicans are standing under awnings watching the show. It looks like an opening scene from "King of the Hill". The power has been out for parts of the town all morning, so the unwashed gringos are crowding into the restaurants for breakfast, and to marvel at the beauty of the weather. As much as I love seeing the rain, it does remind me of the Northwest, and why we moved down here. Grey days are just not as happy as blue ones. But seeing the palm trees brighten as their fronds are washed clean of the dust that permeates our lives here, gives me an appreciation of the miracles that water performs. In another week there will be an explosion of color in the desert as flowers that have lain dormant for the last four years spring to life. I've seen it once before and it is a riot of joy, celebrating life with all its richness. We would do well to carry the analogy to our souls. Pure joy happens when we water the gifts that are hidden within us. It worries me that I get so carried away over just a little rain. Do you think I've gone over the edge?

# Dogs

Dogs have been on my mind lately. It was brought to a head last week when the Princess took our Shih Tzu dog to be groomed. She has been working with the local groomer for four years now. He must be self-taught. No one could be that bad intentionally. Peso came back looking like a chemotherapy victim. With no hair left she looks like a little rat. The good news is that she doesn't realize how bad it is. It's like my grandfather. When grandmother died, grampa did the singles scene. He bought a bright red blazer and put black shoe polish in his hair. He would actually strut as he walked out the door. However he had missed a streak on the back of his head, and looked just like a skunk, but he was a proud one. Peso is pretty much the same. She looks like a rat, but a proud one.

The local dogs are a delightful bunch. The animal rescue has had a spay/neuter program going for several years now, so the population is greatly reduced. They also have feeding stations all over town, so all the dogs are now well fed. They are a hardy bunch. You would think that being wild, they would be mean and even dangerous. The opposite is the truth. They are like their human Mexican counterparts. They're friendly and really appreciate any attention they receive. Anyone we know who has adopted one loves them, and they are great pets. (Donations for VIVA gratefully accepted). I guess it's similar in humans. The mongrels are the toughest and smartest of the breed. It was the pure bred thing that brought down the Egyptian pharaohs.

## Insults

A recent magazine article here in San Felipe referred to me as the "venerable Sam Grubb". Venerable? That means old fart! Am I really that old? To add insult to injury my golf coach, Bill told me that practicing wouldn't help my game. He said, " At your age your muscle memory is not there. You can practice all you want, but it won't change your swing." Well, screw him! I'm not that old. I did practice today, and changed my swing, and it worked! Well, maybe not. Tomorrow I'll play and see what happens. I'll be playing against Bill, and am determined to whip his sorry ass. It is difficult to face the fact that age is creeping up, no rushing up, on me. My hair is white, my strength ain't what it used to be, I sleep more, and just don't have either the ambition or stamina that used to be. Staying out on the town until 9:00 PM is a real effort. That's bedtime. Sometimes I enjoy the comfort that comes with the "golden years", but there are times when I resent the loss of energy.

Old people are often viewed as just someone to tolerate. Someone to be humored. They move slower and think slower, and are not really interesting. I remember some of those feelings when I was younger. You just tolerate the old folks. Now that I am one of them, it's frustrating. I still feel alive. I still have the ability to compete. Still have the ability to be successful in business. I just don't have the drive I once had. Comfort is king in my world. I just don't choose to compete as often as I once did.

## More Traffic

I have a never-ending fascination with Mexican driving practice. Missing car windows are common here, and this time of year when it's cool, it's not uncommon to see plastic covering the missing window. Today I saw a new one. A beat up old car had a shattered windshield. It was totally obscured, so the driver had cut a 12" square hole in it so he could see directly in front of him. You'll have to admit that he had a lot of privacy, and it wouldn't be as cold as removing the whole thing. Yesterday I saw a man walking down the street with a transmission on his shoulder. Do you have any idea how heavy those things are? I doubt that I could even pick one up, but there he was casually walking down the street with a friggin transmission on his shoulder. The classic incident however happened last month. A Mexican friend of ours, a pharmacist, did a U turn out on the highway right in front of an oncoming car. Of course he got hit. It totaled his car, and he is lucky to be alive. He was in the hospital for about a week. Right after the crash, he crawled out of the car and screamed at the other driver, **"Why did you hit me, the ditch isn't very deep here**?"

How's that for rationalization? "It ain't my fault" would be a good country western song title.

# Great Day!

Yesterday turned into a delightful trip around town. My car had a heart attack, or whatever it is that cars do when they don't feel good. We took it to the hospital. That would be Juan. (He's the mechanic who has "Broken Inglish spoken here" over his corrugated metal shed). I had another meeting downtown that afternoon, which turned out to be boring, so I left it. So here I was, downtown, and no car. So just for the hell of it I decided to walk down to Juan's and see if he had looked at it. I know, it was dumb to expect that after only one day, but a little pestering might get the work done before Labor Day. I figured I could call someone to pick me up there. Well of course he hadn't touched the car, and no one was home to give me a ride. Now I was on the far side of town, and no transportation. It was a beautiful day, not uncommon here, and I decided to walk home. It had been at least a year since I had walked through town. Usually it's just drive to where you want to go, do business and leave. What a treat the walk turned out to be! I discovered a new coffee shop that is nice, and I learned that they are famous for their cheesecake. Then I started running into people I knew. There were several small shops that were new to me, and friends in every bar. There were Benny, Sharon and Connie sitting on the sidewalk at Fat Boy's. We had a drink together, and one of those fun, funny conversations about life in Mexico. They are new here, and had just paid their property tax. Their new home is in the million-dollar class, and their taxes for the year were $57.00. They really love Mexico now. After discussing local affairs, the local economy, the Las Vegas real estate market, music, local authors and the benefits of Gin versus tequila, I moved on through town. I stopped at our accountant's office to sign some paper, but she wasn't there, but there is another little bar there and Bob and Michelle were there. We gossiped about some of the seedier gringos around town. Edd (yep, two d's) was there. He does not breathe between sentences and has gusts of up to 120 words per minute. I never hear what he is saying, because I am too fascinated by how he can talk so much, say so little, and never pause to breathe. The main topic was a local masseuse who claims to be a retired Navy Seal with a generous pension. He is always broke, owes money to everyone in town, and survives by having a series of girlfriends who support him for a while. He says that he makes regular trips to China at the expense of the Chinese government to teach healing massage to the Olympic team. Embellishment is an important part of any gossip, and we jumped right in. Between his stories, and our interpretations of it, there is probably very little resemblance to who he really is.

By now we're ¾ of the way through town, and should be home free. Ha! Not even close. I crossed the footbridge at the north end of town and stopped on it to look back at the town. What a pretty sight. The pangas were lined up on the beach in the late afternoon sun, drying their shrimp nets and preparing for fishing trips tomorrow. The shops along the Malecon were beautiful from this distance. They had a wide variety of colors and shapes and really defined "picturesque". So home is only about 5 blocks away. The only hurdle is the Lighthouse Restaurant. I had to walk by that and down the street to our casa. As luck would have it several good friends were enjoying an early cocktail hour on the patio, and insisted that I join them. It may have been the highlight of an already great adventure. Russ was there. He drives a big Hummer. He was sideswiped by a Mexican driver today. The Mexican jumped out of his car and ran. Somehow they caught him. He claimed he was just scared. The Police were going to put him in jail and confiscate his truck. Russ talked them out of that, figuring that if he's in jail, he wouldn't be able to work, or drive to work. So Russ negotiated a deal with the man to pay $100 every two weeks to fix the damage. Russ realizes that he will probably never get the money, but it was his only hope of getting anything. We were very supportive of Russ, well kind of. We did buy him some drinks to help him recover from the trauma. Paco and Robin were there too. They had come down to quietly celebrate their anniversary. They ran into this crowd, and were resigned to celebrate by drinking margaritas. Nate happened to be there too. He is opening a restaurant on our storage company property. He is excited about it, and plans on being open next Monday. The sign out front is going to say "No rice and beans, gringo food only". It will be lasagna, meat loaf, you know, comfort food. His chef has a local reputation of being very good at that. Oh, by the way, Nate just bought one of the local strip clubs too. He is going to clean it up and make it upscale. Somehow upscale and strip club don't fit well in my mind. We gave Nate our unbridled support, and offered to help train the girls. On top of all that it turned out that Nate is a very good country western singer. He wants to join our songwriter's club and be a part of our CD project to record local, original songs. I haven't even mentioned Ken yet. He was a Canadian sitting at the other end of the table, and Beth was there. She explained that she had three e-mail lists. The Christian friends, the seedy friends and the really uptight friends. That's a good idea. There are some things that you just don't want your Mom to see. Especially some of the things that Ken said about Martin Luther King Day. So in spite of vigorous protests that I needed another drink, I headed out to walk the rest of the way home. At this point walking was a good thing, because driving was not really an option.

I don't feel like I have really captured the essence of this walkabout. It was a totally relaxing, laid back bonding event with good friends. It was spontaneous, unrehearsed and aimless but entertaining to experience an afternoon with good friends. It defines one of the greatest joys of living here among relaxed and happy people. I made it home in time for dinner, and it was the most fun I've ever had without becoming a father.

# Staff Meeting

Yesterday after golf, we had a staff meeting. Our staff is a widely diverse, and flexible group. Big corporations could learn a lesson from us. We can solve large problems in minutes, and discuss several topics simultaneously. The regular staff includes a Marine, a banker, a plumber from Canada, a contractor, a greens-keeper, a bartender, an investor, a dentist, and a real estate salesman. During the tourist season, we often have guest consultants. Yesterday the meeting started, as usual, with a discussion of pin placements on the greens, Tiger Woods, and great shots we had performed that day. There was the usual exchange of money. The bets are small, and the penalty for winning is that you have to buy drinks for the entire staff. The bill is usually several times larger than the winnings. The agenda quickly moved on to a discussion of medical conditions. Up for review today were hip replacements, heart surgeries, hemorrhoids as big as prunes (the Canadian), and sore backs. Next was a section on women we have known and would liked to have known. (The astute reader will recognize that the talk about women is all in the past tense. Viagra was touted by one group, while some of the others felt that is would be like putting a flagpole on a condemned building.)

We had a new staff member at the meeting. He just opened a Gym here in town. So the topic of fitness regimes became the highlight of the day. There were widely held opinions on the topic. The consensus was that it's OK to talk about it, but, just like unprotected premarital sex, is not something that a thinking person would actually do. If you are really serious about it, you can join the gym, and plan to work out. Anything beyond that is dangerous to your health. We've all been pallbearers at funerals for friends who exercised. One of the guys had actually looked in the door. He said that there was a lot of strange looking equipment in there. If the Spanish inquisition ever comes back into vogue, that would be the place to hold it. Ten minutes on any of those contraptions would reduce even the strongest man to a quivering mass of jelly, willing to admit to or recant anything. He also noticed that there were no ashtrays by any of the machines, and no cup holders. That in itself should warn anyone about the health risks of actually going in there. That naturally led to expressions of concern that if this sort of things catches on it will lead to someone trying to ban smoking in restaurants. That is as sacred here as the right to bear arms. Well, that's not quite true. The Mexican constitution does not allow citizens to bear arms, but why split hairs?

I was particularly quiet during this exploration. You see, I'd signed up, and actually worked out three times. Talk about feeling guilty. It was worse than being caught by my girlfriend's parents fifty years ago. I didn't want to do that again. The reality is vastly different than the opinions of the staff. You should see this place. It's full of mostly men, but a few women. All of the customers here are white haired, so you don't see those Herculean lifting and straining efforts. What you see are a lot of very weak attempts at working the machines on their lightest settings and hoping that no one notices. With this crowd it's ok to discuss how any years you have been working out, how often you do it and how much better you feel. (All of these discussions are largely bullshit). It's just not socially acceptable to mention what settings you are using on the machines. The room has mirrors covering every wall. It's impossible not to see yourself, and everyone else in the room. The men are the most fun. They look like roosters. They'll be lifting 6-ounce weights like they were in the Olympics. I guess they haven't reached that time in their lives when they realize that it's too late. Young women will not even see them. Of course we have a lot of blue hairs here who are hoping to catch someone's attention. They are generally as invisible to the men, as the men are to young women. I guess life just isn't fair.

The first time I went I wore long pants and a golf shirt, long socks and tennis shoes. MISTAKE! There is a more rigorous dress code here than at a senior prom. Tee shirts, with the sleeves torn off and running shorts are de rigueur, tennis shoes are ok, but must be worn with no socks or short socks. For the really macho guys, a special added touch is to have spandex under the shorts, and the spandex legs must reach just above the knees. The women's dress code is a little more flexible. Sweats are preferred, but spandex or equal outfits are acceptable for women who are under the misconception that they still are sexy. It is not a pretty sight. Self-deception, delusion and denial seem to be essential ingredients to the golden years. Or, as a wise man once said, "Screw the golden years".

One other observation that struck me is how hard they will fight for a parking space right in front of the door, so they won't have to walk far to work out. Then they will drive one block to the bar for a beer or two after the workout. It bothers me when I'm working out that I could actually be doing something productive during this time. Like building a house, or digging a ditch, chopping firewood, playing golf or soccer or rugby, carrying a case of beer from the car into the house, or any one of a million physical things that would actually produce something of value when finished.
 My dirty little secret will never be revealed at a staff meeting, but you know, I really do enjoy the exercise. Go figure.

## Waiting for Spring

I suppose that it's all relative. For people freezing in 30 below weather, spring is still only a faint remembrance. For us here in San Felipe, we expect it to be here later this week. The weather forecast is for high 70's this weekend. It has been barely 60 degrees lately, and for old people with thin blood, that's damn cold! We are running around in long pants, socks, shoes, sweatshirts and jackets. When the wind blows it is just miserable on the golf course. We try to remind ourselves of those less fortunate, but it doesn't work. Those people up in the cold and wet are pretty much on their own. We want warm sunny days! NOW! San Felipe has it's own version of Mardi Gras, and you should have seen the natives. They were all bundled up in ski jackets and wool hats. The bands and the vendors were all stamping their feet and rubbing their hands trying to keep from freezing. The Carnival was still a great success. The local Rotary club sold $500 worth of popcorn Saturday at $.50 per bag. Downtown was full of people and cars. Traffic control pretty much disappeared. Some of the streets were blocked for the festival, but there was no advance notice of the closures. You just had to drive down a street to find out if it was open, and if someone was behind you, you were screwed. Mostly in self defense, and partly just because we have a very cavalier attitude about traffic laws, people were driving the wrong way down one way streets. Especially when things are busy, Mexicans just park in the middle of the street, and wander off. By Tuesday of Wednesday abandoned cars are moved out of the way, and when they remember to remove the barricades, the streets are reopened. That sometimes takes a week of two.

Today I saw someone driving down the wrong side of the freeway. The oncoming traffic just moved over and kept moving. No big deal. I can just imagine doing that in Los Angeles.

# Swatting Flies

It's been a while since I sat down to talk about life here in San Felipe. That doesn't mean it hasn't been as fascinating and busy as usual. Someday I'll tell you the story of how I came home from Calexico without my pants, or of the spectacular desert bloom we are having, or our adventures into the restaurant business. Yes we have been busy and time flies. Speaking of flies, on Sunday the wind was blowing so hard that even the real estate ladies who wear wigs had to stay indoors. (Have you ever seen a blonde wig flying down the street? You don't need my help with that vision. It looks like a little dog being chased by impudent gods.) The wind made playing golf a borderline event. We had a staff meeting to decide whether or not to play and discussed the differences between males and females. That subject was put on the agenda because one of the staff members had just bought one of the local strip clubs. In his report to the members he told us that he was going to make it an upscale establishment. That involved cleaning the mirrors. The consensus among the staff was that we didn't quite understand how you made a strip joint "upscale". We are currently planning a field trip to do further research on the issue, but that will involve some logistical planning that will be complicated by wives who don't always understand the scientific nature of our inquiries. By this time the wind had turned into a dust storm that was blocking the sun. Only one rabid member still wanted to play. We told him to pay for our breakfast and leave. That did it. He didn't leave, or pay for breakfast. By now you may be questioning how all this relates to flies. We're getting there, but it isn't always as simple as it seems. Governmental intrusion into our lives is at the core of what follows. You see, in Mexico you can't buy a drink until 10:00AM. We still had an hour to go, and Bloody Marys were sounding really, really good, so we adjourned the meeting to one of the member's house. He was elected because he mixes killer drinks. So we sat on his partially enclosed patio watching the weather. Partially enclosed is the operational word here. That means that it is a gathering place for flies trying to get out of the wind, and enjoy a little companionship. It soon became a battle for control of the drinks. At one point it looked like the flies were winning. They were giving the little fly finger to the special imported Wal-Mart fly trap we had set up, and heading straight for our drinks. It became hand-to-hand combat. Mano-a-mano. We only had one fly swatter, so we were taking turns using it and doing fairly well until the plastic face on the weapon started to fall apart. Every time we would strike, pieces would fall of the edges. Now, from combat, it turned into an art form. How to strike enough to score, but lightly enough not to lose the weapon. By the time the smoke cleared (a lot of heavy smokers in the room) the patio was littered with bodies on the floor, the table, hanging from window sills, in people's hair and smeared on walls. Scattered among all this carnage were little pieces of blue plastic and we were left with a stubby fly swatter. You can only imagine how we felt. The thrill of victory, the exhaustion that comes after the adrenaline high of battle, the buzz from the second drink. We had won the battle.

As a footnote to the battle, we did lose the war. That afternoon several hundred thousand flies showed up for the funeral, and we were forced to retreat to a more protected fortress. That's pretty much how war works for humans too, isn't it.

## Not Quite Right

Today was a very emotional day. The band that was a big part of my life on Anderson Island sent me a copy of their new CD. Just hearing their music brought back memories of the happiest times of my life. We would meet every week at the Wilson's house to rehearse. Karen would make wonderful desserts (my favorite were the chocolate chip cookies, the male kind with nuts). We would just walk into the house and start playing together, working on songs for our next performance. We would make small talk afterwards (OK some would call it gossip), and enjoy the fabulous dessert that Karen prepared. We only did songs that were a unanimous consent, in fact everything we did was done together. I have never in my life experienced such a close bond with people. The new CD brought back memories of the closest friendships I've ever experienced. What brought tears to my eyes, in addition to the flood of memories, was that they included me on the CD. I haven't been a part of the band for three years at least. They have moved on, and the band has gone to a whole new level without me, but they are still a big part of my life, and they remembered me. That blew my mind. I didn't feel that my contribution had been very significant.

The new CD includes excerpts of some of the introductions I had done to our songs at earlier performances, and the last cut is me singing at what was probably our second ever performance. I left the band because I felt so inadequate. The other band members were superb musicians, and I didn't want to hold them back. The fact that they remembered me and honored my contribution was stunning. I have never felt so honored and loved in my life. It also made me aware that I miss them desperately. My life here in Mexico is about as good as it gets, but it doesn't include the intimacy of those friends. The CD taught me how precious they are to me, and what close friends really are. In a world gone mad with being too busy, and preoccupation with taking, an experience like this shows just how special good friends really are. There is absolutely no exaggeration when I say that this was a revelation and a life changing experience for me today. The word "friends" does not do justice what they mean to me.  Thank you to the new and improved NOT QUITE RIGHT.


With love and affection

Sam

# Letter to Sally

Dear Sister,

Thank you for sharing your adventures of home ownership with us. I am amazed at how smoothly things have been going for you. When they cut down the trees none of them fell on the neighbor's roof and no one was seriously injured. The garage door actually fits without major structural remodeling and no electrical fires were started when they replaced the windows. The plumbing issue won't be noticed for some time, and dry rot is not obvious to the casual observer. The advice you've been receiving from friends shouldn't hurt your feelings. Remember that advice is given in the spirit of jealousy and meanness. They really don't care what color you use.

I would love to come up there and provide my consulting services, but am heavily committed to projects here in Mexico. Perhaps if I explain, you'll feel better about your project. We recently took possession of a house that we sold a year ago. The people who were buying it from us spent a lot of money remodeling it, but the workmanship was terrible and the project wasn't finished. The house was empty for a month between their leaving and our repossession. During that time the local bandidos broke in and stole all the copper wire for the electrical system. They clipped it off at each outlet and at the panel. They got it all, clear to the meter. So now we are paying to have the house rewired, someone else to put bars over the doors and windows, someone else to stay in the house at night until the construction crews put on a new roof, finish the walls, paint it (over the tar that is spilled down the outside walls from trying to repair a leaky roof.). Then we have to repair the water damage inside, repaint that and repipe the propane because they stole that pipe too. Then we have to replumb some of the sinks that never were hooked up. Once that is done we need to finish the office building they started out front. It has no good roof, no doors or windows, no ceilings or electrical fixtures. I don't know what we will do with the concrete block dog kennel they built. By the way, did I mention that the house has no heat, and things freeze here at 51 degrees rather than the 32 degrees you experience up there. Once we have done all those things, plus all the problems we haven't discovered yet, we'll have a house that we neither want nor need. All this happens at a time when property isn't selling well, so we'll probably have to pay someone to live in it until just before the Second Coming.

It's a beautiful house, and it is a treat to be able to do things that are this much fun. Hope you understand why I can't come and criticize your house.

# Northwest Morning

It's a typical gray and dreary Northwest morning. The rain has been drizzling overnight, and looks like it will continue all day. Well we're used to that. It won't depress us or slow us down. Right? Well, maybe not. We're in San Felipe, where the sun shines 360 days per year, but not today. I had forgotten how ugly and depressing this kind of weather really is. It's like an ex-wife. Time makes you mellow out a little over the whole disaster, but you never really think it was funny. Cloudy days are just as miserable as ex-wives. They are mean spirited and don't offer any relief for aching joints or long buried issues of insecurity or unresolved sexual issues.

On this kind of day it's wise to avoid other people. They too will be in a bad mood, and the risk is doubled. You can either say something nasty to them, or they can insult you. A typical conversation would go something like this:

You, "You must have had a rough night. You look like dog poop."

Them, " Your shirt looks like someone threw up on it. Is your fashion consultant a local wino?"

You, "Looks like you've gained a little weight. Add two more pounds, and we can barbeque you."

This is the time that the conversation degenerates into "yo mama" level of insults. Now this is something that happens with close friends. For mere acquaintances the conversation is really rude. Fights, although uncommon, generally happen on days like this. In prisons they can have a lockdown when things are tense. We need something like that for civilians too. No one should be allowed out of their houses, maybe even their bedrooms, and the bars should definitely be closed.

We are the lucky ones. We only have this once every couple of years. I can't imagine how people in other climates manage to survive. You know, it just occurred to me that there are more children per capita here than in the Northwest, by a large margin.

The people up North are probably just too depressed to breed. Understandable. When you are that depressed, it's hard to get hard. Besides, who would want to bring children into a wet, soggy, dark world. Well, it's definitely a survival of the fittest sort of thing. Those of us down here take our hats, and shirts, and long pants, and socks off to you. We admire your strength in the face of such adversity. Keep up the good work.

# The Race

Last weekend we had the Baja 250 off road race here. The race starts and finishes in San Felipe, and it is an amazing show. The town is filled with thousands of racers and spectators. For the week before the race all the big race teams are pre running the course that wanders for 250 miles through the desert and mountains, over hills, rocks through gullies, and up cliffs. Its brutally punishing to the racers and their equipment, and often to the spectators. The big race teams will spend over a million dollars for equipment, cars, huge trucks to haul them and complete repair shops, even chase helicopters to follow their cars from the air. The small teams have a Volkswagen. The big teams set up pit stops, fully equipped at several points on the course in case of breakdowns. The pit stop for one team was a jack, one tire, and three cases of beer. There are $350,000 racing machines, motor bikes, quads, jeeps, this year we even had a Hummer entered. The first prize for all this is $3,500. You would have to be crazy to love the sport, but craziness and love do go together don't they? This year was a smashing success. Literally. The cars that make it back to the finish alive look like they've been wadded up like an old piece of paper. Parts are either dangling, or just missing, and the drivers all look like they've been beat with a stick.

Meanwhile, back in town the entire Malecon is covered with tee shirt shops. I have never seen so many tee shirts in my life. On race day they sell for $15 each. The day after the race the are 3 for $10. Race day is one big traffic jam in town of racers going to the starting line, and spectators heading for their favorite spots to watch. The highway, and all the side roads are nuts. About half the drivers out there think they are in the race. It's this big macho thing and you take your life in your hands to be out there. On the course the fans are just as stupid. They line the course so that they can be close enough to touch the cars as they go by at over a hundred miles an hour. About half the time those cars are airborne and they are never fully under control. One thing that made this year unique was that for probably the first time ever, no spectators were killed, and only 7 drivers had to be airlifted to hospitals. The day after the race is just as nutso. Thousands of people are jamming the service stations, gassing up to leave town. The race teams are pulling out with their big rigs, and most of them haven't come down form the race. They are still driving as if they owned the road, and they are convinced of their immortality, so insane driving is OK.

On the one hand its scary to have an event like this that is so dangerous and out of control. It would not be possible to do something like this in the USA. Officials from a hundred governmental agencies would make sure that nothing went wrong, and that nothing was damaged. Here we don't have all those constraints. We are allowed to do dumb things. There is a great sense of freedom in that. We are not regulated in everything we do, and can explore new things, and entertain possibilities. When things do go wrong we don't try to sue someone. If we screwed up, we pay. It's that simple. Someday Mexico will mature and have all the rules that their older neighbor to the North has, but in the meantime, it's a good life.

# Chilly Morning

This day is starting pretty slowly. The sunrise was cloudless, so not as spectacular as usual, and the wind is blowing, so even though it's 60 degrees, it feels chilly. It just feels a little unsettled. Even Peso, who always sleeps until Diane wakes up, came upstairs to visit me this morning, and just wanted to cuddle for a while. She also wants to play with her golf ball. She bounces it on the tile floor. That reverberates throughout our condo, wakes the Princess, and there will be hell to pay later when she arises. Luckily I have some early meetings, so will be gone by that time. All this started me thinking about family, and the things that make it so precious. (I know, there is no rational train there, but my train spends a lot of time running off track.) It is a special blessing to have little things to remind us daily of each other. I have a Tupperware thingy that holds a pound of coffee that Sally gave me several years ago. I am reminded of her every morning when I make coffee. On cool mornings I put on the shrug that Berkeley made me and it makes me feel my affection for her. I have a picture of Charger on my desk. He's a Labrador who took care of Julie and Tim for years, and shed hair all over me. The act of writing always brings Jill to mind, as does the leather briefcase she gave me several years ago. There is a picture of Lukas leaning over the porch rail at the Anderson Island house that always brings back memories of that family and what special people they all are. The list extends to every member of the family, and the close friends too. What a great blessing that is. Those relationships are what defines me, and gives me a sense of who I am, and the power we receive from our families. Our recent trip to Las Vegas to meet with the Farrell clan was a special treat. John and I have had a close bond since we were small people. ( I have been accused of being a small man too.) We can go for a year or two not seeing each other, but when we do, it's as if we hadn't missed a beat.

So this morning I will head off to work and golf with a sense of community, and a determination to score in the 70's. That has nothing to do with family, but golf is almost as important, sometimes maybe even as much. I am preparing for several tournaments over the next month, and winning is what you play for. As John Murphy would say, "You don't keep score to tell who loses."

# Bancomer

Oftentimes authors will write to relieve stress. By putting it on paper, or some mysterious thingy that only teenagers understand, they can release the anger. It is a good way to keep from going to jail for murder. This piece of writing is an attempt to do that for me.

I hate Bancomer! That is where we do our banking here in San Felipe. Their employees are arrogant, and stay awake nights trying to find new ways to insult and inconvenience me. The abuse they have heaped on me started seven years ago when we first opened the account, and has continued unabated ever since. A list of all the insults would be longer than War and Peace. So in the interest of conciseness and due to the fact that I have a golf game to play in two hours, we'll only relive the last two. Two weeks ago I tried to deposit a check written on a US bank. Bancomer routinely accepts them, but makes you wait for two weeks to credit your account. (The check clears the US bank the next day, so they are using your money for this time, but what the hell). They would not let me deposit the check because the branch manager was out of town for the week, and he has to initial the check before they will accept it. So for an entire week the bank won't accept checks for deposit. OK, I admit that it is a little amusing, and a lot ridiculous, but not a big deal. It's just another wound in the death by a thousand cuts strategy that they have. Now let's move on to the really big one.

After your account has been opened for two years, the bank will give you a debit card. Mine wore out, so one year ago I turned it in for a replacement. Yes, good friends a year ago. Some of the excuses were mind bending. For a while they were out of plastic to make new cards. About two months ago the bank hired a new employee. She has not yet had the formal training session where they show a picture of me and tell all employees to screw with this man. So she went to work on the problem, and finally she got me a new card. When I tried to use it, nada. I went back to her with it, and she looked it up on the computer. **They had issued me a debit card with a zero spending limit**. Simple. Right? Just a few keystrokes and it's done. Not really. She spent a couple of weeks trying to change that with no luck. But she hung in there, and had another card issued. This time she upgraded me to a **gold debit card**. However it too was issued with a zero spending limit. This has to be the ultimate in bad credit, when your debit card has a limit of nothing. She called yesterday to tell me the problem is solved, and I can pick up my new card today. I am somewhat suspicious about what will happen when I show up.

I have not detailed the crap that I've had to endure from some of the other arrogant assholes that work there during this process. Without Elizabeth, I would surely be locked in some Mexican prison for the rest of my life. At my age however, it just might be worth it.

# *Angus*

Angus was a great dog. A little black Scottish Terrier. He spent his entire life taking care of Dan and Audrey. He would loudly announce any visitors, and attempt to intimidate them, but his wagging tail was a dead giveaway that he didn't have a mean bone in his body. When the Coffmans brought home the puppies, first Scarlett and then Moose, Angus trained them. He taught them how to manage people, and totally disrupt a formerly quiet home. His patience with what amounted to his grandchildren was exemplary. Through all this he also taught Dan and Audrey about kindness, and tolerance. Well, that may be an overstatement. Maybe it was just tolerance. Angus was in charge. It was his house, and anyone else there served at his pleasure. He had the gift of making the act of waiting on him seem like he was doing you a favor.

Angus accomplished all of this with a kind and loving disposition, in spite of health problems that would have made any human being cranky at best. He was not a complainer, even when he was hurting. He set an example that would be a great model for us to emulate. We miss you Angus.

Last week Angus passed away. In a way it has to be a relief. He suffered more than he deserved. Dan buried Angus in a beautiful spot, and we had a guy sort of funeral. Dan, Bill and I sat down on Dan's verandah spoke briefly about Angus, then we drank beer and swatted flies. By the time we were through the deck was littered with little fly bodies, and a few beer cans. Angus, you are one of the boys and will always be in our hearts.

# No Coherent Message Here

Well, it's been a while since I wrote to you, so today we'll try to catch up on some of the miscellaneous things that have been happening here in out little village. A month or so ago was Semana Santa, or holy week. It's as big as Christmas down here. It's at least a four-day holiday for the Mexicans and about 50,000 of them come down from Mexicali and Tijuana to camp on every level space in town. They cover the beaches and vacant lots all over town. Last year I even saw a tent pitched on the roof of a house. Bimbo is the company that makes the Mexican version of Wonder bread. They had semi trucks parked overnight here to restock the little tiendas selling food. Hundreds of locals put up taco stands and beer trucks come down in caravans. One year we opened our garage door to run errands and there was a family asleep in our driveway. San Felipe is actually a suburb of Mexicali, although 120 miles away - so we are largely ignored by the government up there. However, they spend about two months before the holiday sprucing the town up. They pave a few blocks of streets, sweep other streets and paint a few curbs. This year they sent down a truckload of stop signs. The crew didn't want to go to the trouble of removing worn out ones, so they just randomly picked intersections and planted the new signs. They are still there. We now have stop signs on dead end streets, obscure intersections, and several on the main streets of town. I guess that's progress. We still don't have a traffic light in town, but who knows, that maybe on the agenda for next year.

Yesterday was the annual chili cookoff. It was a mob scene. We even had a team from Australia this year. There was a blues/rock and roll band there keeping the noise level close to permanent ear damage, and lots of old fat women dancing. One was so fat that when she hauled ass she had to make two trips. I almost rushed up to her and put a tongue depressor in her mouth because she looked exactly like she was having an epileptic fit. When our bodies age, our minds sometimes don't notice. If we only knew how ridiculous we look. On the other hand, we often don't care what it looks like. We're still having fun.

Well, I better go now. We're having a batch of people over this afternoon for a pool party. That means Diane has her knickers in a twist getting ready. I still don't understand the concept of cleaning a house before a party. Especially when everyone will be out in the courtyard. But being a good husband (survival technique) requires sharing that concern, cleaning stuff that doesn't even look dirty and making sure that the party setup is absolutely perfect. A couple of drinks and the courtyard will be a shambles, but our house will be clean, and more importantly, it's the day before the housecleaners come. We wouldn't want them to have to clean a dirty house. By the time the party starts, we'll probably be too tired to enjoy it. I will rely on being fueled by alcohol to maintain a sense of balance and order in an otherwise unruly and chaotic world.

# *Freaky Weather*

Wow! I can't believe what's been happening around here the last few days. The wind has been blowing so hard that the palm trees look like the hurricane pictures you see on TV. If you can picture small Chihuahuas, straw hats and large tents flying down the street, you understand what we're talking about here. After playing golf in it we were covered with sand, in our hair, ears, and other sensitive areas. There is a brown haze that surrounds us from the ongoing sand storm. The dirt penetrates solid stucco walls and covers everything in the houses. Cars with completely closed windows have a fine film of dust covering the entire interior. I've discovered that it really pisses women off when you write your name in the dust on their coffee tables. If they would just wait a couple of hours, a new layer would obliterate the writing. This morning the temperature has dropped like a rock and it's a chilly 60 degrees and cloudy. Well, not totally cloudy, but enough to make the sun have to dance around to find open spots. It's sending shafts of light radiating from its center through holes in the clouds fanning out trying to warm this chilly earth. Global warming, my nalgas! Today we'll have to wear long pants and maybe even a sweater. No big deal, you say? HA. That violates our God given right to wear shorts and tee shirts. It upsets the basic, fundamental rhythm of our lives. The human suffering is almost intolerable. No trips to the swimming pool today. We'll probably have to have a cocktail party just to survive. Well, OK, maybe that is a little extreme. We'd have the party anyway.

Peso and I are going to be bachelors today. Diane is going up into the mountains in search of Pai Pai Indian pottery. She has put together a deal with a local art gallery to sell their pottery, to help them survive. They live pretty primitive lives up there, but make beautiful pottery. Hope this works out for her. More importantly, I hope I don't get in too much trouble with the boys today. Being unsupervised all day can be dangerous, especially at the staff meeting we have after golf. Some of those guys are a bad influence. That's why I like them so much. But they do think differently than women, and wives struggle to understand what in the world we were thinking when we try to lob golf balls over the pro shop, and dent a few windows. The pro doesn't quite understand either, just like the restaurant manager gets crabby when we order pizza to be delivered to his restaurant. Sometimes we do get lucky. Our wives don't find out what happened until a long time later. By then some of the sting has worn off, and we only have to do penance for a few days.

## The Purpose of Life

What is my purpose in life? This question is usually asked by people who are depressed, or have recently had "bad" things happen in their lives. I've thought some about the question, but can't become too intrigued by it. Who really cares? My answer, if you can call it that, is it doesn't matter. The whole point in being stranded here on this miniscule dot in the universe is to enjoy the moment. If you have seen astronomers on TV explaining the size and structure of the universe you know that even our solar system is too tiny to amount to much. We are a part of the Milky Way. It is so large that since the beginning of time our solar system has only rotated around it 18 times. That is a fact that will help you bore the crap out of people at cocktail parties, or encourage guests to go home early. The point, however subtle, is that anything we do is so tiny that it would be difficult to notice from a radius of more than a few kilometers, let alone outer space.

So if what we do doesn't matter much, why do anything? Exactly! Now we're closing in on the big picture here. A good exercise is to contemplate the happiest times in our lives. They are not working our butts off and achieving public recognition. They are time spent alone on a beach, time spent just being with a loved one, or doing something that makes someone else feel better. A touch, a kiss, OK sex too is good. It's those casual moments that make our lives precious. Happy people are not the ones who spend 4 hours a day commuting, and working long hours. Happy people are the ones who choose doing joyful things to enrich their lives. They improve their lives by trading car payments for independence. The beauty of this lifestyle is that it's contagious. These are the people who shed light on the lives of those around them. So, in the narrow sense of it, they are the least productive of our citizens. But, in the broader sense, they are the ones who enrich our world.

Happy New Year. My resolution for the year is to do less and enjoy it more. Hope it works for you too.

# Just A Newsletter

I haven't written in a long time, so here is one of those letters that
used to be so popular around Christmas where a parent writes a
letter telling how incredibly talented their children are. Hope this
isn't quite that boring. The biggest news here is rain. We had two
nights in a row last week with vigorous thunderstorms. The
lightning was beautiful, the thunder the loud rolling kind, and
strong winds driving a heavy rain for about half an hour each
night. Between them they gave us our annual rainfall of about 1".
That happens so rarely that no one is ever prepared for it. We were
lucky. No damage, just water all over the kitchen floor. Many
homes were flooded, and all the dirt streets overlooking downtown
were flushed away. It will be a long time before some of them are
passable. All that dirt washes down to the main street, plugs the
storm drains, such as they are, and creates a big lake that floods the
businesses. The shops that don't get flooded are usually damaged
by the roof leaks. We have rain so seldom that no one thinks about
rain when building roofs. So a little rain creates a mini boom in
the roofing business, and hours of telephone conversations and
cocktail parties to discuss who was damaged. By now the stories
have been embroidered with the lace of exaggeration to give them
more character.

On another note, we hear in the media about all the violence in
Mexico. Well, it's a little different here. Some friends came home
one evening and found a burglar loading their stuff into his
pickup. When he saw them he quickly unloaded the stuff back into
the house, said, "I'm sorry." and left. It's both a sweet story about
the people who live here, and a sad story that so many are so poor.
The economic slowdown hits them harder than most, and they are
the last to reap the benefits of a recovery. Hopefully an improving
education system, and better support systems will help alleviate
these problems. I have great faith in the quality of people here,
and faith in their futures.

As I told you in my last letter, I'm trying to retire again. It's
working. I have done nothing worthwhile in 3 weeks. Have read 6
books, swam every morning, gone to the beach with Diane and the

dogs, and worked a little on my Spanish lessons. Have learned a ton, but still not conversational with the language. Have been working with my successors at the storage company, and am quite comfortable with the transition. We meet once a week to review important things, like logo shirts for the employees and a new marketing program that is showing some results in improving business. Haven't been playing golf, other than a trip to the driving range, and don't really miss it too much. I'm sure I'll get back into it as my energy returns. Am adjusting well to a frugal lifestyle for now, but who knows what the future will bring?

Love,

Sam

## Hunting With Hoot

One day, a long, long time ago, I was a teenager, full of all the
usual male adolescent stuff, and becoming a man. I was well on
my way, because for $70 I bought my first car, a 1941 Chevrolet.
Most of the paint had been worn off of it, so I painted it. Knowing
nothing about painting, I went to a store, bought paint and a brush
and plunged in. I painted the bottom half black, and the top half
yellow because those two colors were on sale. The color choice
was also a form of rebellion. I did it just to irritate my Dad. He
rose to the bait, and made me repaint to top half, so I went and
bought pink paint. Over the next several months the pink faded, so
it was kind of yellowish pink. That was a great old car. Flat out it
did 74 miles per hour, but I put the entire JV baseball team in it
when the team bus wouldn't start. We made it to the game on
time, but lost to some Jr. High team. That was just about as
embarrassing as our uniforms. They had no budget for JV
uniforms, so they made us wear old pants from the football team
and our own tee shirts. No logos, no hats. You can imagine how
silly that looked, football pants, with no pads under them. Anyway
I drove the car for three years, paid no attention to maintenance
issues, largely because I didn't know about them, and it never quit
on me. And, just owning a car gave me status with my friends,
especially those who didn't have cars yet.

Owning the car is probably why Hoot Gibson invited me to go
duck hunting with him. Now I'm not a hunter. I've done it, and
support those who like it, but it just never has given me any thrill.
But, for some reason, probably that male thing of not wanting to
admit that I wasn't a hunter, I agreed to go. I didn't own a
shotgun, so I was the backup. Incidentally, if you've never eaten
wild duck, don't. It tastes like fish, is tough as nails, and there
isn't much meat on one. Just go to the store, buy a chicken and
you'll have a far superior meal without the misery that is required
to shoot a duck. You also need to know that duck hunting is only
done in the late fall, when the weather is cold and miserable, and
instead of chasing them you huddle and wait, which makes the
cold even colder. Well, I started this paragraph to introduce you to
Hoot. His father was a well to do junk dealer, so they lived in a

big house. Hoot was basically a fat, lazy rich boy. The only reason we hung out with him was that he had a cool tree house, and could afford to buy candy for all of the guys. His older sister was hot. That helped, but she ran off and got married when she was 16. That took her off our list of potentials, but that is another story. I've lost contact with Hoot, and have often wondered what happened to that family.

Anyway, Hoot and I headed out to some property that his Dad owned clear out in the middle of nowhere. It had a duck pond, about 50 yards across, and they had a little wooden dingy about 6 feet long, and not very stable. When we arrived Hoot got all excited because there were about half a dozen ducks floating and just hanging out and quacking over some duck gossip. We bundled up in our heavy jackets, insulated boots, and about 30 pounds of other clothes and launched the dingy. I was manning the oars while Hoot sat there with the shotgun. Hoot just sat there and I asked, "Why don't you just shoot the damn things?" He explained that you couldn't do that. You had to wait until they started to fly, then you shoot. OK, so I paddled all over that little pond chasing them, and they just casually swam around ahead of us, and wouldn't fly. Among his natural gifts, mensa candidate wasn't one of them. Hoot ran out of patience, and stood up. As soon as he did that, I knew that nothing good was about to happen. He braced his feet across the dingy, which was rocking precariously. I was doing acrobatics with the oars trying to keep us upright. Hoot took aim at one of the mallards which was only a couple of feet away, and fired. From that range, the duck just disintegrated. We didn't have time to see that though. The recoil from the blast flipped the boat, and dumped us in the water. I still remember the shock. An icy duck pond in November is colder than an Eskimo's nose. Now we are fighting for our lives. Luckily the pond was only a couple of feet deep, so we were able to trudge along through the mud on the bottom and make it to shore. We were wet, shaking wildly, cold to the bone, and 20 miles from home. If you've ever seen how bedraggled a wet cat looks like, you have a picture of us. I don't remember the drive home, and don't remember much about Hoot after that. Our male bonding days were over. I do remember wondering why anyone would actually do something so stupid, when you could be sitting in a nice, warm house eating civilized food, at a fraction of the price that you pay to go hunting.

It was 20 years later that my father-in-law talked me into going duck hunting for the second time. That was a much better experience but anytime I've hunted something really big has gone wrong. This trip was no exception. We went out early with his buddies. Sat in a blind, just long enough for the cold to attack us. Then we returned to their little clubhouse, drank gin fizzes and watched football. Unfortunately, while we were out there someone shot a goose and my father-in law volunteered to take it home and clean it. My mother-in-law had just bought him a duck plucking machine. It was a round drum with little rubber fingers all over it. You just ran the goose through it and the fingers plucked the feathers. The machine was brand new, and this was it's first performance so we set it up in the middle of the kitchen, shoved the goose into it and stood back to watch the show. What a show it was! When the goose came out the other side, there were no feathers on it, a perfect job in just minutes. (If you've ever tried to pluck one by hand, you know that it's a tedious, messy job.) However, there were feathers in every room of their rather large house. You have no concept how many feathers a bird has until you float them all over your house. The women were having a reception at the house that afternoon, and the women panicked. There we were, the entire family madly running around the house chasing goose feathers, and us men trying to avoid the wrath of the women we loved. For years after that we would regularly find little goose down feathers in the furniture, and on bookshelves and in the clothes. I guess it's just the little things like that that have dampened my enthusiasm for the sporting life.

# Dog Training

It's been a slow week here in San Felipe. Summer is here and swimming has become almost important as cocktail parties. Diane just brought home a 4-week-old Chihuahua puppy. She's almost all black, with just a little white spot on her chest. Her name is Peligrosa, which is Spanish for "dangerous". OK, so she is a cute little dog, and although adventurous, not yappy. She doesn't realize that she is small, so will attack anything, including the other dogs here. We now have 3 Chihuahuas and Peso the Shih Tzu living here in the complex. The owners have all agreed to turn the dogs loose in the courtyard, and every day prior to cocktails and swimming we have a dogshit patrol. It's a good bonding experience for us humans, the dogs love to watch us picking up their poop. It sets a festive mood, and inspires the dogs to avoid constipation. They don't want to feel left out and love the feeling of pride that comes from making a contribution.

Speaking of being left out, Peso will not acknowledge the presence of the puppy. She turns her head the other way when the puppy enters the room, and leaves the room if the puppy tries to play with her. Now, as you may realize, people who leave their homeland, and take up residence in a third world country are usually just a little off center. That's one of the things that makes living here so special. Sunday, at a birthday party, we met a woman who talks to animals. Diane immediately scheduled a counseling session for Peso. They had their first meeting today. The woman was all prepared. We had to send her a picture of Peso two days ago, so she already knew what was going on in Peso's mind. Peso told her that she liked to swim in the ocean, wanted more time on Diane's lap, that she would like things to be more calm around our house, but she did like it when we had company. She enjoys sitting on the top of furniture backs. She also told her that we didn't have to get rid of the puppy, but Peso wanted to be in charge of training the puppy. This will be fun to watch. If Peso won't go near the puppy, how is she going to train it? Obviously I am pretty slow when it comes to this sort of thing. I will keep you posted on how the training progresses. Hmmm, wonder if we could hire Peso out as a dog trainer. She could earn money for her dog food.

This afternoon Diane had the puppy out in the courtyard while she was swimming. Peligrosa managed to climb up on the ledge, and jumped into the pool. She is a natural. She swims just like a bowling ball. She sank all the way to the bottom before Diane could reach her. We thought "Aha! Now the dog will know not to do that." WRONG! We fished the dog out, turned her loose, and she did it again. Peso, in the meantime, was enjoying the show, and hoping we would just leave her there on the bottom. I am more convinced than ever, that Peso has no future as a dog trainer. She might do well as an animal control officer.

The other big event is that we have formed the "La Ventana Golf and Screwdriver Team". After two months of intense negotiations we have agreed on the shirt design and have ordered them. We considered mauve, taupe, and cerise, but settled on red. Long sleeves were rejected, not based on style, but because it's just too hot for them. George wanted ruffles, but lost on a close vote. The logo is a golf club crossed with a swizzle stick. Our team plays twice a week. We have to play 9 holes because the bar doesn't open until 10 AM. By the time we finish the 9, the bar is open and we have screwdrivers. While drinking, we have a staff meeting that covers topics as diverse as Aztec art and bathroom jokes. The Aztec art doesn't take long. The focus of yesterday's meeting was how to deal with ear hair. Jim is thinking that estrogen may be the answer. We're all encouraging him to try it. He may be onto something big, or maybe something really small. We promised to tell him if we noticed his voice getting higher. He's already overweight so enlarged boobs will be hard to spot. We haven't mentioned the experiment to his wife, but we're sure she'll be pleased if he no longer has unsightly hair in his ears. We meet again tomorrow, and I'll let you know what big problems we solve then.

# *Nacho*

Nacho is the nickname for Ignacio here in Mexico. We have a dear friend who is saddled with that nickname. He's the greenskeeper at our golf course and about 60 years old. Hs life story is worth telling. His grandfather was born in the USA and took care of the horses for a rich family on Santa Catalina Island. He was kicked by one of the horses and lost an eye. The family gave him several bags of silver dollars to compensate him, so he moved back to Mexico and raised his family there. Nacho's father was born before they moved back to Mexico, but was raised as a Mexican. When the father grew up, he jumped the fence, walked through the desert, and survived the ordeal. Which was no small feat. Lots of people die trying to cross the desert at the border. He made it to his sister's house in Los Angeles, where she told him that he didn't need to have done that because he was already and American citizen by birth. So Nacho, although born in Mexico became a Naturalized citizen. He grew up working the fields until an uncle offered him a job working at a golf course. He took the job, not even knowing what a golf course was. He worked on the crew for several years, and when it came time for promotion he was turned down because he didn't speak English. He went home crying that night, and signed up for an English course. He spent the next year learning English and today his English is flawless. He fell in love with the golf business and the game. Every day after work he would practice and eventually spent 6 years playing successfully on the Mexican professional tour.

Nacho married young, as is quite common with Mexicans, and had three children with his wife. When she was 24 she passed away and the youngest child was only one year old. Nacho has been married to his second wife for 33 years, and he is so grateful that she helped raise his children. He says that she did a great job an he would do anything for her. His career has led to golf related jobs in Tijuana, Cabo, San Diego, and now in San Felipe. All during these years his wife has lived in San Diego raising children, and now devoting her life to grandchildren. He goes home to his family only about one weekend a month. He lives in a little trailer here in San Felipe, and sends most of his money home to the family.

Nacho is also a very talented chef. He has been to our house several times to cook us a Mexican meal. WOW! It is undoubtedly the best Mexican food you will ever eat. He brings all fresh ingredients, and spends about 4 hours in our kitchen moving fast the entire time. There is always a fine soup, and then varying dishes from beef to fish to shrimp to pork. We live on leftovers for most of the following week, and it is a big treat for us.

Nacho is a small wiry man. He is totally dedicated to his golf course and has wrought miracles with it. It is one of the most beautiful courses you will ever play. He's modest, and a delight to play with and a good coach. His golf tips have improved my game a bunch. Not a smart thing for him to do, because we bet against each other. His tips have cost him some money. It's an honor to have him as a friend, a kind, generous, unassuming and gentle man.

## Sermon On The Beach

In a few weeks I'll be going up to the Northwest to visit my family. I love all of them dearly, and feel so blessed to have such a close bond with my sisters, children, grandchildren and a few very close friends. However, a part of me doesn't want to go. Leaving our little village is never fun. Life here, thanks to our Mexican friends, is just so perfect. Things that at first looked primitive to us, begin to make more sense as we adjust to the new culture. One of the most dramatic differences is the lack of consumer credit here. The average person has no access to credit to buy a car and mortgage money does not exist for most Mexicans. Recently, a few American companies have started making mortgage loans, but they are focused on resort areas built to US standards for US buyers. That explains why so much housing here is substandard by our measures. I recently talked to a friend here, and he explained to me that his main goal is to complete building a house for his wife and children. His reasoning was that if something happened to him, they would have a place to live. He said that it is a real struggle for a family to survive is they have to pay rent. Over the past several years he has managed to build a small kitchen, a bathroom and two bedrooms for his family of seven people. That is the Mexican version of life insurance. A little scary perhaps, but they don't have the stress of trying to make the house payment every month. It's the same thing with cars. They drive old cars, and often have them wired together to keep running, but they don't have car payments. It's always a shock to me when I come North to see all the expensive cars on the road, and to see the intensity with which they are driven. A large percentage of the Mexicans don't even have a car, but they manage to get to where they need to go by riding busses, hitch hiking, and the ubiquitous ride in the back of a pickup.

Without credit their living expenses are dramatically reduced, so they don't need to drive themselves into medical problems trying to make the payments. Instead, they are a kind and gentle people, who live much richer lives than their US counterparts. In the US the houses are bigger, the cars shinier, and people are much more driven. Even relaxation requires spending money in the industrialized world. For us a major social event would be a horseshoe tournament on the beach including a picnic of wonderful homemade food. That isn't to say that they don't work hard. They do. But they don't do it with the pressure that interferes with health and productivity that typifies big city life.

Mexico is moving forward. Someday the banking system will straighten out and start loaning money. Someday businesses will become more efficient, and government will become more pervasive. I'm doubtful that it will make life any better than it is now, and it is difficult to call that progress.

## *Dogs and People*

I've been thinking, always a dangerous thing. It's time for me to define happiness. I'm too old to waste time doing things that don't point in that direction. For me it starts with being connected. It's crucial to feel like of part of the world. We need to be part of a family, a community, a world. Finding those connections is a lifelong journey. We can take some big steps in the right direction by learning from our pets. We have a new puppy. She poops wherever she wants to, and doesn't give a tinker's damn about how we feel about cleaning up after her. She demands attention when she wants it, and ignores us when we call her. Just how often would we invite a friend to our house if that's how they behaved? I can hear the conversation now:

"Honey, let's invite the Gross family over to dinner. She's so cute when she pees on our new carpet."

"Well, dear, I don't know. The last time they were here she chewed up one of my shoes and he tried to hump my leg."

"I know. Weren't they cute? But I was a little taken aback by their fight over the food at dinner. There was plenty for everyone, but they just had to have each other's plate."

Well, you get the picture. The difference here is expectations, and acceptance. We expect puppies to behave that way, and most importantly they love us no matter how we behave. Unfortunately, we do the same things with our friends. We create a model, and expect them to behave to the standards we have set for them. Usually they have no idea what our expectations are and when they don't match our view, we become hurt, angry, jealous, and all those other negative emotions. We then start criticizing them, both internally, and to others. We've now separated from them, and the rebuilding process can be anywhere from painful to impossible.

I'd like to suggest another model. Why don't we accept who they are, appreciate what they do that makes us happy, and forgive what doesn't? If we could be more like our pets, what a great world this would be. It's not always easy to think like that. Comments like:

"He doesn't sweat much for a fat guy." Or

"He sure screwed that up, but he did it thoroughly."

are not quite what we're talking about. But, you can work out your own style. The important thing is to practice accepting and loving those around us. It makes us feel better about ourselves, and I believe that it helps make our friends and family better people too.

Thanks for listening, and I love all of you just the way you are.

# Leroy

Leroy never ceases to amaze me. He is just like those energy saving light bulbs they have in motel rooms. There is a delay between flipping the switch and any light appearing. When the light comes on it is too dim to be of much value. He is a regular member of the staff meetings we have after golf. Two weeks ago we were sitting in the bar reliving our round of golf before starting our regular agenda. We were discussing just how beautiful the 16th green is. It sits on a hill overlooking the beach. The view is 360 degrees of the Sea of Cortez, miles of beach to an overview of the course with the mountains in the background. I had just casually mentioned that it was a magical spot that would be a great place to get laid. Leroy didn't say much at the time, but apparently someone flipped his switch, and the light came on. Now Leroy is also a very open, creative man. He has lots of ideas. Unfortunately, very few of them work. Once the light comes on, the off switch seems to malfunction. So Leroy got it in his head that he wanted to "live the dream" as he put it.

Never one to procrastinate, or to spend much time on details, Leroy took his girlfriend out and lubricated her with a fair amount of tequila, and convinced her to go out to the 16th green around 11 o'clock that night. The green is surrounded by little hollows covered with lush grass. At night, and he picked a full moon, it has to be about as romantic a spot as can be found anywhere on earth. There are no houses nearby so privacy is not too much of a problem, unless the people next door at Pete's camp are using binoculars. (Our local rumor mill will confirm if anyone was watching within a day or so.) So far the plan is working well and the girlfriend has no clue what led to this, but she's impressed at how creative and romantic Leroy is. You can just imagine her beginning to think wedding bells and babies. It was at this point that the plan started to unravel. In Leroy's own words,

"Sam, did you know that the sprinklers come on at 11:10 PM?"

Well, they do, and that really dampened the mood to say the least. The girlfriend started screaming. They jumped up trying to gather wet clothes and escape the drenching. Once out of range of the water they head back toward their car, 489 yards away (it's a par 5) carrying their soaked clothes. Once again in Leroy's words,

"Sam, did you know that they have security people driving quads around the course at night?"

Well, sometimes a dream should just remain a dream. I admire and envy Leroy for his initiative, and somehow feel a sense of disappointment that it didn't turn out as planned. It would have been an inspiration for the whole staff. Keep on dreaming Leroy. We're behind you all the way.

## *Beautiful Morning*

5:45 AM: The horizon has just turned the bright orange that signals the beginnings of a brand new day. The palm trees are moving lightly, promising a light breeze to go with temperatures in the high 70's. The sea is still asleep laying flat and quietly across the expanse from the Baja to the mainland of Mexico. It's the perfect time to drink the morning coffee and reflect on nothing and everything.

Today I'm going North to the big city, which is a good reminder to me about my basic values. Here in our little village we drive old cars on dirt roads, live in small houses (Well except for some of the rich gringos). Credit card debt is a foreign concept to the locals, and sharing what we have is a way of life. Going to the city is entering another world. Too much traffic, frantic pace, stressed out people who have mortgages, car payments, family expenses, and a population that is focused on being civilized. By their definition that is a material driven world. I don't mean to sound too negative about all that. There can be great satisfaction in competing in that world, and being successful. The lesson that I've learned in the last few years is that both approaches are just fine. For some of us, a simpler approach to life is rewarding in itself. Giving up some of the perks that money brings and forgoing good streets and reliable phone service alters one's view of what is important. After a while the idea that all third world countries are somehow deprived becomes patently wrong. Living a happy life, as long as the basic necessities are met, becomes the standard of measure. Both worlds are just fine, but it isn't necessary to try to homogenize them In our village a stressful day is one in which you become occupied with details and miss the siesta, or even worse, miss spending time just sitting around with good friends and doing nothing that has immediate value.

6:45 AM: Sun's up! Wow, it's beautiful. It's completely quiet and still and you can hear the town begin to stir. You know, maybe, just maybe, I'll fix some huevos rancheros for breakfast. A big meal always makes me a little lazy. Yep, that's the plan. The trip North will have to wait until, well, it will just have to wait.

# Gringos In Mexico

Here in San Felipe there is a fairly large gringo population. It's mostly retired people, and most of them are a little off center. I guess if you're normal, you stay home as you age. It takes something special to move away from family that you love and move to a third world country. Even though it's a fairly quiet village, relatives do worry about our safety and often question our wisdom and sanity. There is probably some validity to their concerns because the culture has different values, and even going to the bank can be dangerous. Gentle, patient, healthy people have been know to keel over from heart attacks while trying to deal with the incompetence and bungling of the banking system. If they make a mistake, which is common, they charge you for it. But that isn't what I started to tell you about. There have been a couple of gringo incidents here recently that highlight the cultural differences between our countries. The first involves a friend who went to church last week. If you knew them you would understand why this is news. They moved down here a couple of years ago, and have assimilated very well. They have lots of friends, both gringo and Mexican. It's worth noting that most of their Mexican friends are bartenders and waiters. I have no idea what prompted her to attend a service, and doubt that she does either. Anyway, she went to church. During the service the man next to her lit a cigarette. (Only in Mexico, right?) She was so stunned that she dropped her beer.

Have you ever noticed that these crazy things seem to run in families? Just last week her son came to visit from LA. He's a bright young man with a nice wife and daughter. He is a successful businessman, good golfer, great guitar player and quite outgoing. Seemingly a very nice man. Well it turns out that well into the cocktail hour (actually that should read "hours") he told me that he'd just had a physical exam before he came down to visit. The Dr. did the usual blood pressure, pulse, listen to his heart, etc. Then she told him to drop his pants.

When he did she said, "Ohmygod, you need to stop masturbating"

He turned red and said, "OK, but why?"

She said, "Because I'm trying to examine you."

I guess the definition of normal is someone you don't know very well.

# Good Friends

"You never know what you got till it's gone". Remember that song? OK, name that tune, the singer and songwriter and year, and you win. You won't know the prize until it's gone either. Well, if you twist my arm, the prize is a beer, that I'll drink for you. I hope we have multiple winners here. If we don't have winners, I'll just drink the beer anyway. The thing that brought this song to mind is that last week I received a CD from the band that used to let me stand on stage with them. It has been four years since we played together, and they are still going strong. I've often felt that my leaving took them to a whole new level and the new CD is living proof of that. Their harmonies are amazing! I played golf several years ago with Don Felder, who used to be lead guitar for the Eagles. He will have that honor for the rest of his life. I now feel the same way. I was the original rhythm guitar for NOT QUITE RIGHT. When they become famous, I will pretend that "artistic differences" led us to part. (We won't mention that my moving to Mexico had a lot to do with it.)

There is a point to all this, and we are getting closer to it. Be patient. On the new CD they have used clips from my introductions to songs lifted from earlier performances, and have included a cut of me singing, "I Was Born Ten thousand Years Ago". I remember that performance well. It was outside, in the rain, under a little tent at the Anderson Island Fair. It was our biggest audience to date, maybe fifty people, several of whom actually listened to us. The band started gradually during a series of potluck dinners. A little jamming led to a few evenings just to play together. That evolved into a casual rehearsal process. What held it together was the Wilsons. They would host the evenings, and Karen would make these fabulous desserts. (My favorite being the boy style chocolate chip cookies, with nuts). Over the next year or so we decided to become a band, hired a crazy hippie to give us private lessons, and to come over on occasional Saturdays to teach us how to play together. The driving principles for the band were that we would never play for money, and when it stopped being fun, we would quit. That was ten years ago, and they haven't quit yet. We bought a sound system after performing outdoors one day. We were lined up on a porch, so we couldn't hear each other from one end to another. On one song we finished a full measure apart. That's why you see speakers on stage pointed back at the musicians. We met faithfully once a week for several years. We all loved the practicing together, doing only songs that were a unanimous choice. We became a very tightly knit family. We did a couple of performances per year, and some of us had to take anti stage fright drugs to get up there. It was exhausting to be up there in front of a packed community center trying not to make too many obvious mistakes. It was also exciting to see the audience clapping and stomping and cheering. We made a lot of memories together. Our biggest fan passed away, and we were invited to play at his funeral. We played at weddings and private parties, but were never asked to play a bar mitzvah.

The bonds that we formed were the warmest, closest feelings I have ever had with friends. They were indeed family. What has brought tears to my eyes is that after all these years they remembered me, and included me in their CD. I have never been so honored or touched in my life. Thank you my compadres. I still miss you more than words can tell.

# Another Sunrise

It starts with the subtle bit of grey intruding on the black of night.
It is whisper quiet as the world holds it's breath waiting for the
morning show. Suddenly, a gusty wind springs up as the tide
changes. The wind charges in like a colt, bouncing around
buildings, ruffling the palm trees impatiently telling them to wake
up. It pulls the laundry off the neighbor's line, scattering bras, tee
shirts and jeans around the dust that covers our world. Yards here
in this little village are usually very plain. Landscaping consists
of a cactus plant and a rock, so the clothes are dirty all over again.
Not yet content with the damage, the wind blows a fine dust
through solid block walls to cover rooms that were dusted just
yesterday with a fine brown coat. The Sea of Cortez makes a
gentle hissing sound as if telling the wind to be quiet. It's too early
for all this noise and energy. Inadvertently, the wind blows away
the blanket of humidity that has descended on the village like a
stifling blanket, and gives hope of a comfortable day ahead.
Meanwhile as the sky starts to gently start to glow in anticipation
of sunrise, you can see the clouds like lumps of mashed potatoes,
without salt or garlic, scattered about on a platter, leftover from
some celestial banquet that was held to honor the moon last night.
Finally, the sun appears bringing with it its palette of colors to
embellish the sky and clouds and then paints the complex
combination of civilized and natural elements that define our
material world. In a matter of minutes the sea, the mountains, the
village and its inhabitants begin to radiate a colorful glow that
foretells another day of blessings. At the same time the gods clear
the table of the detritus of last night's fiesta, and the clouds fade
away, waiting until tomorrow night to return to the sky. The sound
of the first car floats around the neighborhood heralding an early
riser on his way to work, trying to complete his tasks before the
afternoon heat wave descends to suck the energy from all the
living creatures in our little desert town. So, as the morning show
slips into daytime, and the world starts awakening to the day
ahead, those of us who have been spectators smile, and feeling
nourished begin our daily routine. But we are changed by the
experience. You cannot watch this show without a feeling of awe
and a belief that there is a higher power guiding our lives. The

challenge for us humans is to avoid being spun into daily crises and lose the magic that sunrise brings.

As the sun rises, so do the inhabitants who can't afford to flee the heat of August. They sit up, stretch, yawn and put their feet on the floor to start their daily chores. One of these people is Reuben. He is a bumper car in the arena of life. He careens from one adventure to another, enjoying the smooth moments in equal measure to the crashes. He enjoys every moment of the ride, with no fear of what may be next. Reuben draws pleasure from every moment, and has perfected the art of not planning ahead. Reuben is an upholsterer who has recovered just about everything in our house over the last 5 years. He's had a small shop down by the traffic circle for years. It was right on one of the main streets, an ideal location for a retail business. Last May he showed up at our casa with his new girlfriend. Although she didn't speak English, we managed a pleasant afternoon with her and by the time they left the Princess had hired him to recover a couch on our patio. That always requires some negotiations, and a significant down payment, because he never has enough money to buy material. We're now halfway though August, and until last week we hadn't seen him all summer. That's not unusual because we know he doesn't live on the same planet as we do. About two months ago we noticed that he had moved out of his shop, and there was no sign giving any clues as to his whereabouts. We didn't worry about it though, because he's reliable in a very flexible sort of way. Finally one day we spotted a sign pointing to his new shop. After driving around for a while, we found him!! His new shop is in the Gavilonnes, a modest residential area. It's down a dirt path that requires a 4 wheel drive vehicle to climb out of the potholes and over the humps. You do have to keep moving though, or you will sink into the loose sand. We found his new shop! There he was proudly sitting on a box, smiling as always. After exchanging embraces and a warm welcome, he proudly showed us his new place. The new office is a two bay RV port. Dirt floor, no front doors and the electric meter is mounted on the side of his outhouse. In one bay is his sewing machine looking rather lonely sitting out there in the middle of that big space. The other bay had an old Dodge van. The odds of the van ever moving on its own power are somewhere between slim and none. He's cut a hole in the side of the van and installed an air conditioner. That's home to Reuben.

Oh, I forgot to mention that Reuben wasn't wearing a shirt or shoes. That's a little unusual even for him. He is always smiling, and always wearing a clean tee shirt. After a little casual conversation the story began to unfold. Reuben's wife lives in Mexicali, about 120 miles away. He used to go visit her about once a month. She must have found out about the girlfriend about the same time the girlfriend found out about the wife. He was a little vague on the details, but the result was that they both threw him out. He was laughing as he told us that between them they had all his clothes. The jeans he was wearing were his entire wardrobe. So we went back home, grabbed some old jeans and tee shirts and took them back to him. He was happy to see them, but a little puzzled that we had seen his semi-nakedness as a problem. Wouldn't we all love to know how it happened that he had to escape without clothes? We may never find out. This is normal stuff for Reuben, and he doesn't see what all the fuss is about.

No we don't have the couch covered yet, but with any luck we will hear some more adventures as we try to encourage him to complete the job. We have learned a lot from Reuben. He lives a good, if somewhat random life, and enjoys the ride. I'm beginning to think that may be a lot more productive than being serious.

# Brilliant Thoughts

I woke up this morning and thought it would be a good day to think brilliant thoughts and write them down. That's like practicing yoga. It immediately clears my mind from any thoughts at all. Then what starts to come to mind are a bunch of things that have happened recently (Could be a case of long term memory loss). Our lives consist of a plethora of random events, some tragic, and some amusing, and a lot of them in between. It's how we react to them that gives them the flavor that makes this world so fascinating. For example, I take the dogs out every evening to a little enclosed space for their evening constitutional. Peso has been doing this every evening for several years now, but every time, she walks into the area, then stands there just looking around. It used to irritate me. I just want to go to bed, but she's in no hurry. I remind her to hurry up and she looks up at me with a surprised look on her face. She looks like the boy from the TV show Two and a Half Men. Totally clueless. You can just watch the reaction on Peso's face, "Oh yeah, I forgot that's why we came out here". Then a bird flies by, and Peso is once again distracted. Once again I remind her, "Do you want to sleep with your legs crossed?". She has that surprised look on her face again, "Oh, sorry, I forgot." We finally get the job done. Now the dogs are in a hurry to get back to the house for a treat. You have to admire them. They do get the job done, and only become focused when there is a reward.

That's not a bad philosophy. Just going through life with nothing on your mind, until something comes up that inspires you. In the case of the dogs, they are at the mercy of their keepers. In our case we're at the mercy of our own thoughts and actions. A great reminder for me are the stop signs here in our little village. Once a year, just before Easter, they send a pickup load of them here, and a crew installs them around town. The installation is governed by where it might be easier to dig a hole, so in many cases there will be stop signs planted on a main thoroughfare where it is crossed a little dirt road. As the year progresses, trees and bushes grow up and hide some of them, and a lot of them are knocked down or stolen. No problem. Next Easter they will bring another load to town and replant. By that time there aren't many intersections where you need to stop. For the locals it does present somewhat of a problem, because what you thought was a stop is no longer one, but you adjust. Surprisingly, that doesn't seem to cause many accidents, just a lot of close calls. You also need to add to the mix that the minimum driving age seems to be the ability to look through the steering wheel, and driver's Ed. hasn't been invented yet. These drivers often take a casual approach to formalities like stop signs or one way streets or lane designations. Traffic enforcement is just a little lax too, so tourists are often a little amazed and sometimes intimidated by the freedom of expression that characterizes traffic flow. Our little village doesn't have enough traffic to make that a hindrance and it is entertaining, to say the least, just to be in the middle of cars turning at random and unpredictable intervals. On top of that turn indicators, mirrors, windshields, fenders and doors are factory options that are often not chosen for a lot of the cars here. Repairs are handled differently here too. Someone sideswiped my car a couple of weeks ago. (Stopping to exchange information is optional too) They broke the driver's side mirror. Instead of ordering a new one, the shop just took an old piece of mirror, cut to the approximate size of the old one and glued it on. It's pretty rough around the edges with little cracks and flaws, but it works, and it cost $8.00.

So while in many places driving is a chore, and often frustrating, hard work, here it's an adventure to be enjoyed.

The moral of all this, if there is one, is that accepting the little things, enjoying them and sharing them with friends is what makes a truly good life. Brilliant thoughts will have to wait for another day.

# Peppers

Early this spring the Princess bought a pepper plant, and put it in a pot on our deck. The little bush grew and is now covered with little red peppers about the size of a small pencil eraser. We were spending some quality time together this afternoon. She was directing me while I watered the plants. The kumquat tree is full of little ones, and the lemon tree is doing nothing. The basil is trying to go to seed, and the rosemary is making an attempt to take over the entire deck. The plumeria stick that Kent gave us is growing leaves now, and soon we will have those fragrant flowers that the Hawaiians use to make leis. The mint has died, but we keep watering it, hoping it will come back. Then we arrived at the pepper plant and gave it a drink. The Princess asked me if I thought the peppers were ripe yet. Now, two weeks earlier Miguel had been at our house and he tried one. He said that it wasn't very hot, so I thought, "How bad can it be?", so I picked one and took a tiny bite of the tip of this very tiny pepper.

HOLY COW!!! I spit the piece out and ran for the water. No help there, my mouth was still on fire. I dashed upstairs to the kitchen and fumbled through the cabinets, frantically looking for some crackers. (I had seen in an old Western movie 30 years ago that crackers will soften the burn.) Finally I found them and just tore open the wrapper. No time to peel back here, fold over and leave the package ready to reseal. Just dive in tear open the crackers and stuff them in my mouth. At last! A little relief. The cracker thing really works, sort of. Most of the searing pain subsided, and I once again thought that it might be OK to continue living. However, my lips were still numb, and didn't recover for several hours. Remember how it feel when you go to the dentist, then have to wait a couple of hours while your face thaws. This was a similar experience, except this was inside my mouth and except that this really hurt! My lips were numb in a painful sort of way, then they started tingling, still hurting, and gradually tapered off. This all happened a week ago and my mouth starts to hurt just thinking about it.

Peppers are one on the basic food groups here, and we pride ourselves on using them liberally in our cooking. We are experienced professionals at the art of eating peppers. We have hardened taste buds that revel in the challenge of a good hot pepper, but these little bastards are not normal. I am convinced that they have been genetically altered by some alien force to make them totally inedible. I could have died had I eaten the whole one, instead of just a tiny nip.

We're now faced with a problem. We can reject out of hand some of the options, such as ever considering eating one of them. Cooking with them would be equally foolish. Taking the bush to a toxic waste dump would be dangerous. They could cause an explosion of catastrophic proportion. I think we'll just put crime scene tape around the deck, and try to move on with our lives.

# It's a Changing World

Life here in our little village is changing due largely to events in the world that really are beyond our control or even influence. For the developers who focus on selling property to gringos, it has been a disastrous year. The bad publicity from the U.S. press about violence and swine flu has virtually dried up their market. That frustrates all of us here because we don't even have violent crime in most of Mexico, and the swine flu has never appeared on the Baja. It has meant financial hardship for working families, and even bankruptcy for many small businesses. It's just not right or fair, but I guess that's life, and we find ways to adapt. In spite of all the negativity there are some positive things happening. There is still a steady stream of foreigners moving here for the good weather, safety, and cheap living costs that still exist. There are others who are moving here because we have so many good cocktail parties and people who are a little off center. We still have a relaxed atmosphere without the stress that seems to be a part of life up North. It is a very healthy place to live.

The most fascinating result of all this change is that the Mexicans from Tijuana, Mexicali and Ensenada have discovered San Felipe. San Felipe is on the water, so it is much cooler than Mexicali, and yet warmer than the often chilly Pacific Ocean side. There are large crowds who show up on the weekends to enjoy a weekend at the beach. They arrive with their luggage strapped to the tops of their cars, pitch their tents on the beach and have fun. Our beach has been deserted since we moved here 9 years ago. This year, for the first time, we have families picnicking on the beach, playing soccer and volleyball and swimming n the Sea of Cortez. It's great to see such a beautiful place being used and enjoyed by so many people. The Mexicans are well behaved, polite, open and friendly and a pleasure to have around. They are entirely different than the people who come down from the States to party, and be loud and obnoxious. The Mexicans also have different spending habits.

Some of the local merchants, who have relied on the tourist business, call our new visitors the "sandwicheros" because they often bring their own coolers with food, rather than visit the sit down type of restaurant. However they do spend money. The taco stands and small Mexican restaurants are doing a strong business. The affluent Mexicans, and there are a lot of them, are renting or buying houses or condos, and they do spend liberally.

Now, I have no empirical data to support my theory, which is a euphemism for saying I have no idea what I'm talking about, but there is a huge opportunity here. It requires a fundamental shift in thinking from focusing on the foreign investor, to concentrating on adapting to the preferences of the Mexican citizens. There is a large population on the Baja who have significant amounts of disposable income. Some are even rich. However, if you want to do business with them there are some basic changes that a merchant needs to make. First and foremost, learn Spanish. Although most of the Mexicans do speak English, they are much more comfortable using their own language (duh). To them it is arrogant of someone doing business in their country who refuses to learn their language. (again, duh). This may require business to hire more Mexican employees, but our experience is that with positive management, training and encouragement they are superb workers.

The second basic thing is to learn to do business in pesos. Again, insisting on dollars is a slight to their National pride. The peso is a reasonably stable currency, and in fact over the next year may prove to be stronger than the U.S. dollar. Businesses that think in dollars quite often are niggardly on the exchange rate they use for pesos, so may be actually increasing their prices by 3 to 5% to anyone paying in pesos. Pricing strategies based on peso thinking could very well be more stable than dollars, and will certainly earn the respect of local consumers.

Finally immerse yourself in Mexican culture. A promotion celebrating the U.S. victory over Mexico in the Mexican American war will not be very effective here. Semana Santa, or Day of the Dead promotions, on the other hand, could be very successful here. A genuine respect for Mexican culture will affect how you inter react with your Mexican customers. I also suspect that the more you become involved in the Mexican community, the more you will respect them as a generous and kind people.

The economic turmoil affecting the world right now is creating an opportunity for us to think about who we are and how to prosper (not just survive) in this unstable world. Always remember to save the earth because it is the only planet with Gin.

# Thoughts On Retirement

I'm an old retired guy, sort of. Began thinking about the concept
when my sister announced that she is retiring at the end of the
year. One common theme with us retired people is how to make
the money last as long as we do. As our bodies age, we lose the
stamina to abuse ourselves the way we used to. A side effect of
this is that we tend to get healthier, although crippled by a series of
minor injuries and ailments. Occasionally we stumble into good
health care, which further exacerbates the problem. So now we
become a problem to society, because we live too long, and we are
usually obnoxious, bothersome people to have around the house.
So with all the vitality left in our bodies we start plotting and
scheming for way to scam more money to support a moderately
lavish lifestyle. (Moderate in that we go to bed at 9:00PM). Here
are some business plans I'm working on:

1.    Send out a letter in an appeal for money, just like the ads on
TV for the hungry children. Us older people want money to
travel, irritate children, drugs and alcohol. We will guarantee that
at least 10% of the money will be used to help old people make a
wish. They'll never fulfill them, but that's not our problem is it?
The other 90% of the money will go to administrative expenses
(my salary)

2.    Another approach could be to invent and sell products that
appeal to older people. For example curling irons for ear hair, and
braiding patterns for nose hair. One of our friends is working on a
design for a tire that pees on dogs that approach his car. Maybe we
could market a combination product that can act as either a cure for
diarrhea or constipation. It would appeal to people who can't
remember which they are. Obviously, I could use some help here.
The rapidly expanding population of old people has to create
opportunities for products that have little value, but sell well

One of the problems with any of these ideas is that it would require
some effort to make them work. That is a really big problem. Just
the thought of making an effort makes me tired, and just now my
back has started to ache. Maybe we could just boil the whole
process down to its essence. Cut through the crap, get to the

bottom line, get down to brass tacks. I could offer a lifetime guarantee and VIP benefits to anyone who just sends money. No products will be shipped to you. No one will call on you. No one will even care who you are. This is a completely hassle free offer, and shipping and handling are not a problem if you wire the money. Hope to hear from you when we return from Italy.

# *Animals*

Harold left us yesterday. It was a bittersweet parting for me. We had become attached to him. Harold was a young pigeon who landed in the enclosed area where we walk the dogs. He showed up about two weeks ago, probably having left the nest before he was fully flight certified. We first noticed him when the dogs found him, huddled behind the skeleton of an old suauro cactus. He spent most of his time huddled back there. We fed him bread crumbs and oatmeal, and tried to keep the dogs from sniffing him to death. Having Harold there created some major challenges for us. The dogs were so intrigued with him, that we had to have numerous conversations with them to re-focus them on why we had brought them out there. Doggy constipation was an imminent threat to our living room carpet. Between that and having to feed and water Harold, he was indeed a bother. The last few days he was here he started wandering around the courtyard, so the dogs, upon entering, made a mad dash around the courtyard looking for him. What ensued was pretty much a period of thrashing around while Harold ran for cover, and we ran around trying to herd curious dogs to the other end and remind them to pee. The dogs would get that look on their faces that said, "Oh, yeah, I forgot about that". Finally Harold has left to do whatever pigeons do. We do miss him, and wish him well.

On an entirely different, but tangentially related topic, we had dinner with some Mexican friends this week and over a bottle of fine red wine, they began telling stories of Mexican folk lore. Most of the conversation was lost in the wine, but one story did stick, sort of. Before telling the story, you need to know that this folklore is centuries old and over the years has gained legitimacy with a good share of the population. It is not told as a fairy tale, but as the truth. The story is about a snake that lives mostly in southern Mexico in the more tropical areas. They call it a milk snake because it can rise up and attach itself to the teat on a cow, and drink its milk. People have reported seeing as many as four of these snakes attached to one cow. That isn't the best part though. When nursing mothers are asleep in their hammocks, the snakes will climb the tree and then slither down the hammock and start nursing the mother. You would think that would upset the baby, but the snake has that figured out too. Yup. You guessed it. The snake slips its tail into the baby's mouth to keep it pacified while it steals the milk. Internet research, by others, has discovered that snakes are allergic to milk, so it isn't possible for this animal to exist. Well, OK, if you say so. But I prefer to believe the charm of the tale.

I just can't remember the story of the man who turns into a frog at night. We'll have to invite our friends over and take notes next time.

# A Mexican Moment

This is a story that perfectly describes life in Mexico. It's a story of overcoming poverty, ingenious and creative thinking, generosity and the gift of enjoying life even in the face of adversity. There are two players in this little story, one gringo and one Mexican. Let's start by meeting the gringo. Robert has been living in our little village for several years now. He is a very talented construction worker. Robert does great work on plumbing, electrical and concrete projects and can fix just about anything. He is young, strong and loves doing things that put his body at risk. His spare time is spent driving around in the desert on his quad, a small 4 wheel vehicle and he's usually alone. He has had a number of crashes and mishaps, but so far has survived and made it back to town. You may remember a couple of years ago I told you the story of him riding in the desert after smoking some funny tobacco and losing his clothes. When he got back to town he realized the problem, and luckily was able to retrace his steps and find his shorts. That's pretty normal stuff for him. We could spend some time reliving some of his mishaps, like the time he was out on the highway, miles from town, and sideswiped the Mexican version of Greyhound. The list of incidents is fairly long, and entertaining, but derails us from our mission of describing the latest mishap. Let's just say that Robert is a kind, generous, talented man who sometimes doesn't use good judgment.

The other half of the story spins around the Mexican, Juan. San Felipe is the town where old cars go to die, and Juan has one of them. It's an old pickup with no hood, all of the body panels are crumpled and the headlights and windows disappeared a long time ago. But it still runs, sort of. It's the kind of truck that you only put a couple of gallons of gas in at a time so that if it does die, you won't have a full tank wasted. I don't know much about cars, but I think it might be the fuel pump that wasn't working that day, so Juan siphoned gas from the tank, puts a little in the carburetor, drives for about ½ mile, stops, reloads the carburetor, and goes again. On this day he was making the 120 mile trip from Mexicali to our little village. It was a slow trip, but it was a nice day.

Now here comes the part where these two strangers meet and help each other. Robert's quad had broken down again, not an uncommon occurrence. Luckily, this time he was close to the highway when it happened. So Robert was beside the road when Juan came by. Here's Juan struggling to get his crippled truck back to town, and he stopped and offered Robert a tow. So they hooked a rope to the quad and away they go, ½ mile at a time.

Now Robert is pretty creative himself, and he had some plastic tubing with him. So he rigged up an IV for the truck. They ran the tubing from the jug of gas in the cab to the carburetor and when the car would start coughing, they would stop squeezing the tubing long enough to fill the carb again. With this system they sailed all the way into town. There should have been a victory parade. I wasn't there, but I can just imagine them grinning from ear to ear as they arrived home.

What a great story! Most of us would have had to call a tow truck, taken the truck to a shop for computer diagnosis, and spent a week or so waiting for a new fuel pump. In any case we certainly would not have been offering to tow someone else in the middle of our predicament. It is this generosity of spirit and sharing of what little we have that makes the Mexican people so special, and make it such a blessing to be able to live here with them.

# Cooter

Cooter is one of the boys. (With a name like that, how could he not be?) He occasionally plays golf with us on Thursdays, and with him it's a physical sport. He doesn't just hit the ball, he attacks it. He has been seen swinging so hard that he pulls himself completely off balance and tips over. When these things happen to him, which is quite often, we try to give him support. Randy lovingly refers to him as that spastic son-of-a-bitch. The beer that he uses to keep his muscles relaxed may be a contributing factor in his excessive flexibility. Last week he went down so hard that he swallowed his chew. Cooter may lack a little in refinement, but he more than makes up for it in entertainment value. He's the eternal optimist, and is convinced that he understands women. (That should give you a clue.) Management has finally allowed him back into the clubhouse after the little incident last spring when he told the waitress that she reminded him of a wrench, because every time he saw her his nuts tightened up. At the very least his speech is colorful. He is definitely a good old boy.

Cooter always has a plan. No matter what the problem, he has a solution. Neither the plans nor the solutions ever work , but that doesn't deter him. He just keeps charging forward. He's just crazy enough that someday one of his efforts may actually work, and he will get rich. We all doubt it and the boys give him about a million to one odds of him ever doing anything right. Some of his current projects include a tire that when a dog approaches, it pisses on the dog. He hasn't worked out the details yet, but it's probably the most promising of his inventions. He is also excited about his idea for a new beer. He was at our regular meeting after golf, where we discuss the game, money changes hands, drinks are served and refilled, and we solve world problems. Once we had solved the health care system problems of the USA, Cooter could contain himself no longer and jumped in. He was raising investors for the latest project. He was preaching to the wrong pew, because our group lives a rather modest life style due to a lifetime of bad financial decisions. Anyway, he is a visionary, and details escape him. His new idea was to make a beer called "Responsibly". The way Cooter reasoned it, he would not have to spend a dime on advertising. Every liquor ad on TV already says to drink Responsibly. By this time the third round of drinks was just a memory, and the boys looked at Coorter in awe.

"Cooter, I think you done it" said Ray. "You finally come up with a winner". There was a short pause while all this sunk in.

Then Billy asked, "How much does it cost to build a brewery?" Again, a long silence. No one had a clue, but Cooter was ready for that one.

"We don't need one. We just buy a bunch of Bud Light and change the labels. And here's the topper. I figured out the labels. We have a guy on the porch holding a beer in one hand and a condom in the other. Get it, responsibly? We'll win awards with that one"

By now things were getting a little fuzzy around the edges, but I was dazzled by the enthusiasm and the impeccable logic. I put $100 on the table, and said, "I want to be the first investor". That drew a round of applause, but no more money.

Well, the next morning while shaking off the cobwebs with morning coffee, it occurred to me that buying beer at retail, and relabeling it and distributing it for sale might have some problems. Like how would we make any money at it? There also might be an issue with Budweiser objecting to the plan. Oh well, I've paid $100 to go to concerts that were not nearly as entertaining as Cooter.

# *Bailey*

We already have two dogs who totally dictate and dominate the rhythm of life at our house. Peso is the Princess. She will not lower herself to play with other dogs. In the presence of other animals she will actually lift her nose in the air and turn her head away from them. When she is sleeping, she will not tolerate being awakened, and when she wants to sit in your lap, you are expected to sit. When Peso wants to play fetch, you are expected to fetch for her, and if you want to eat, you better share it with her. People only exist to cater to her whims.

Peligrosa on the other hand is very outgoing and sociable. She is the head of the entertainment committee, and spends all day organizing us for events that amuse her. She will eat anything, to the point that she has been poisoned twice by finding something she shouldn't eat. She is actually a pig in a dog suit. So between the two of them, feeding them, taking them out for walks several times a day, catering to their whims and pampering them, it doesn't leave much time for a life of our own.

Just when you think you have it figured out, something happens, as stated in the first of Murphy's laws. Yep, it happened here two days ago. A friend (Or at least she used to be) had to make an emergency trip back to the States for three weeks. That left us with a third dog, Bailey. He is a tan dog of questionable breeding, with just a hint of Chihuahua. Bailey is two months old, thinks housebreaking is something that burglars or unruly children do, and needs to have someone next to him all the time. When you take the dogs to the big outdoor doggie bathroom, ours get right to work. Bailey sits at your feet, looking at your with big, brown eyes, pleading with you to pick him up so that he won't have to walk all the way back to the house. As soon as we return to the house, he pees on the floor. I know he does that out of some deep seated psychological need to piss me off. (Sorry about the pun) For Bailey the morning starts at 4:00AM. He starts crying loudly, demanding attention. That means taking him outside so he can check things out, then coming back into the house and playing tug-of-war with one of your socks that he has retrieved from the laundry. That is followed by him jumping into your lap and biting you with his sharp puppy teeth. After about an hour he curls up on your lap and goes to sleep. Then you can finally put him back to bed for another hour before the process repeats. I must admit he is an affectionate, sweet dog, but he is wreaking havoc on our household. We've pulled up all the rugs so that his frequent "accidents" (Ha! They're not accidents. He does it on purpose.) are on the tile floor. I'm convinced that he excretes twice his body weight per day. (Buy stock in a paper towel company. We're using a roll a day.) Our privacy or convenience are not on his agenda. Yesterday I was sitting on the john with my pants around my ankles. Bailey forced open the bathroom door, marched in, climbed into my shorts and fell asleep. Remembering the old adage, "Let sleeping dogs lie", I must have sat there for over an hour, waiting for him to wake up. I never realized just how uncomfortable a toilet seat can be.

We're well into the second week now, and his owner hasn't contacted us once. We are beginning to wonder if she has skipped town and left us with this charming nightmare. Bailey and Peligrosa have become inseparable. They spend the entire day chasing each other at a dead run throughout the house, jumping on the furniture, leaving a path of destruction in their wake. They eat together, take naps together, play together and spend time just looking cute together. They have become best friends and if Bailey does finally go home, both dogs will have a hard time adjusting. I'm sure you can see where this is going, and it's scary. We will be sacrificing what is left of our lives to these little animals, and they are way smarter and more controlling than we are. We are totally over matched in their presence. Well, as they say, "One day at a time". I think I'll have a gin and tonic and try to remember if raising children was this hard.

## Trevor

Trevor is a Canadian who came to our little village to visit friends for a couple of weeks. He's been here six months now and is looking to buy property. He is only in his mid thirties, and his body is held together by a series of titanium pins as a result of a logging accident. He's never been married, and often tends to make questionable decisions in choosing girlfriends. That probably explains his extended bachelorhood. He attacks life with enthusiasm, often not tempered by common sense. His first night here was spent in jail due to an argument with some tequila and the local police. Mexican jails are every bit as bad as their reputation, and the police are sometimes not too sophisticated in their treatment of prisoners. It cost him all of his cash, and several hundred more dollars to retrieve the car he had borrowed from the police impound. The cell is crowded, filthy, cold and they don't feed the inmates. You would think that might discourage him about staying here, but Trevor's mind doesn't work the same way as most people. He is still, however, a little nervous in the presence of law enforcement. Everything that Trevor does, he does with intensity. In spite of all his injuries he is a superb golfer and can spend hours just practicing. He is the epitome of entrepreneurship. He created a job for himself doing landscape work at the golf course. Even with his battered body, he can still spend all day loading and unloading rocks by hand to create gardens. The developer doesn't have the money to pay him yet, so he is working on a handshake. He just has the will to make it work. In short he is tough, hardworking and smart and a good man to call your friend. The fact that he careens from one minor disaster to another just enhances his appeal. That brings us to the reason for this letter, Trevor's Christmas.

Trevor went to friends house for Christmas dinner, and there was a Mexican couple there with a one year old baby. They forgot to bring the diaper bag, so asked Trevor to hold the baby while they went home to retrieve the bag. Now Trevor is many things, but family man is not one of them. He's very good with dogs, but children are foreign to his world. He only had to watch the baby for 10 minutes, but that's all it took. Just as soon as the parents left the baby peed through his diapers and wet Trevor's pants. Before Trevor could react, the baby threw up a large burst of curdled milk all over him. I wasn't there but can just picture him at this point. Panic had to be the first reaction. He was holding the baby at arm's length, looking for help. The baby is also soaked, and covered with vomit, and no one there wanted to touch the mess. Trevor may be inexperienced, but he is a man of action. By the time the parents returned he had the baby naked, holding him out over the bathtub. The baby is screaming while Trevor is trying to figure out how to hose off the baby. It was a thoroughly shaken Trevor who gladly handed to baby to two concerned parents. As in everything that Trevor does, there is a bright side to this experience. None of the locals will ever hire him as a nanny.

# *Moonrise*

People often, me included, often wax poetic about the stunning beauty of the sunrises here. There are usually a few clouds over by the mainland to add color to the ceremony of gradually increasing light and burst of energy as the sun clears the horizon. There is no question that it is a magical, even sacred, event that plays out every morning. Right now the sunrise is at about 6:37AM. I work on e-mail, and miscellaneous stuff awaiting that time every morning, then go out on the deck to watch the show. I have discovered that it is much more exciting if you have coffee in your hand during the performance. It is a quiet time, surrounded by beauty and a sense of the vastness of the universe. However, the sunrise is not the only magical moment. There are another few magical moments that occur for several nights of the month, and that is the moonrise. I don't understand why we don't give it the same reverence that we give the sun, especially during the full moon.

When the moon first breaks the horizon, it is a deep orange and stays that way as it rapidly rises into the night sky. As it appears, it casts a moon path across the water that seems to generate more light than the moon itself. The rise is a smooth, seamless process that can only produce a sense of awe as you watch. When it first appears it has that dark orange color and seems much larger than normal. As it rises it slowly turns to the yellow that we are used to seeing, seems to shrink a little, but is still beautiful. The moon path across the water brightens and widens and almost turns night into day. Incidentally, December was a "blue moon" month. That is one of those rare months when we have two full moons. It's better than a Christmas bonus at work. Also incidentally, moonrises don't go well with coffee. They are much better with gin and tonic. It is, however, these special moments that make life so beautiful and give us that sense of wonder that cleanses our souls.

There are a lot of beautiful things in our world. We just need to take a moment to appreciate and love them to restore our faith and inspire us to create passion and beauty in our lives.

# Parenting

As we look back on our lives, we all seem to share a common sense of inadequacy in our parenting skills. No matter how dedicated we were as parents, we wonder what we should have done better. We beat ourselves up with thoughts like, "I shouldn't have spent so much time working." Or, "I shouldn't have taken that vacation without the children." "I shouldn't have been drinking in front of them." Occasionally our insecurities are reinforced by visits with them and they start telling us what they remember of their childhood. That is always a shock. The things that impressed them the most are invariably things that we don't even remember. Then there are the sessions when they tell us about the things that they sneaked by us. Just take me out and shoot me! Where did I go wrong? I didn't know. I must be a really bad person to have traumatized them so badly. OK, you have the picture. If you have several children, like we do, the list of transgressions is even longer. The problem with this thinking is that it's not supported by the results.

When we look at how they turned out, it's pretty much a miracle, but they usually turn out just fine. The ones who do succumb to drugs are about the only exception. There does not seem to be a formula for predicting the success or failure of children as they grow up. Children who have grown up with model parents sometimes fall apart, and children from broken dysfunctional homes often are very successful in building productive and happy lives. Even more puzzling is the disparity between children from the same litter. We have, as do most families, children who are doing fine and a great source of pride. We also have some who break our hearts.

Most of our children, in spite our perceived shortcomings, remember us fondly, and do love us. (I'm speaking here of children in their late 20's or more). We won't talk about the teen years here. Those years are universally a disaster for parents. The point to this rambling is to remember that we did what we could in face of a totally incomprehensible task. No one has yet discovered a fool proof method of parenting, and no one knows how to be perfect. We are who we are, we did what we could, we still love them, and who could ask for anything more?

# *Uncle Charlie*

As I approach my golden years, some would say that I've passed them by, it is fun to reminisce about the people who have meant so much to me over a lifetime. One of the most special of those is Uncle Charlie. He's actually my brother-in-law, several years younger than me and one of the kindest men to ever walk the face of this earth. He is also somewhat of a free spirit, which is what makes him so interesting. Maybe we should illustrate with a few of his finer moments. Rated in the top ten of the memorable things that Charlie has done was the weekend at the beach. We had gone down to Seaside to the family beach house to relax for a few days. It was the first vacation I had taken as an adult. We had my wife, our baby, and Uncle Charlie. It was early spring, and the house had been empty for a couple of months, so it was cold and clammy. The first thing we did was light a fire in the fireplace, unpack, then sit down to have a beer. Just then a neighbor came knocking on our back door with a funny look on his face, so I strolled over and opened the door for him.

He said, "Did you know that your roof is on fire?"

All hell broke loose about then. We rushed upstairs, which was just a big dorm with several beds. The roof was an old cedar shake affair, and flames from the burning shingles were just starting to drop onto the beds. The upstairs had a half bath with a small sink with a tiny spout. I rushed back down the stairs and grabbed a bucket and started running up and down the stairs throwing buckets of water on the beds trying to hold off the flames. Charlie, who was in his early teens at the time, found a little juice glass. He would run into the upstairs bathroom, turn on the water, fill the glass, turn off the water, then go pour the water on the burning beds. We were starting to lose ground when the local fire department showed up and very efficiently put out the fire. All during this, with firemen running all over the house, Charlie keep at it with his juice glass. He looked like something from a comedy skit on TV. This all happened almost 50 years ago and is still a vivid memory to those of us who were there.

Several years later, through a series of odd coincidences, we ended up owning a Sunfish, a small sailboat that could handle two people at the very most. One cold spring day I took Charlie out on the lake to teach him how to sail. It went rather uneventfully until we tried to dock. The wind was blowing right at the dock, so the strategy was to head just about 10 feet to the right of the dock going full speed downwind. At the last second I was going to do a hard U-turn, dump the wind from the sail and end up beside the dock. My big mistake was to fail to explain all this to Charlie. He panicked when we headed full speed at the shore, and he tried to climb the mast. MY GOD, THAT WATER WAS COLD! When we went in, my glasses fell off and went to the bottom in about 10 feet of water. We crawled ashore and ran to the house rapidly turning blue. I am blind as a bat without glasses, but there was no way I was going back in for them, so we gave an 8 year old neighbor $20 to go retrieve them. He thought that was great. He was too young to realize how cold the water really was. I don't think that Charlie and I ever sailed together again.

A couple of years later Charlie joined the Army. Not a good decision for someone who was not inclined to follow rules. He was stationed in Guam, and came home on leave after several months there. On the way back to Guam, he stopped off in Hawaii for a couple of months. One Sunday evening he decided it was time to go back to work, so he turned himself in. The MP's told him to go away and come back on Monday. So a couple of Mondays later he turned himself in and was shipped back to Guam. Once there he was court marshaled and confined to base for 6 months. On Guam there isn't much else besides the base, so Uncle Charlie figured what the hell, and stuck it out.

Uncle Charlie is married now with a nice family and a job. He still has that independent spirit and in his own words is, "Still looking for the golden scam."

# Boxing

Who would have ever thunk it? I have never been a fan of boxing. I'm just not a fan of violence in any of its forms. I guess you should never say never. There is a family here that have become just like family to us. They have four children, one grown boy, two teenage boys and an 8 year old girl. The entire family is nice. They are hard working, including the kids, polite, and generous. They don't have much, but they have each other, and the parents do everything they can to provide opportunity for the kids. Manuel is 14 now and has been boxing for several years.

The local boxing club is an impressive volunteer organization. They work the kids hard, but are very careful to avoid situations where someone might be hurt. When they have matches with the big cities of Mexicali, Ensenada, Tijuana etc. our little village wins most of the fights. Polite behavior and respect are demanded of them. The kids wear big padded headgear and fluffy gloves. The fights are three rounds, and if a fight appears to be one sided, it's stopped immediately.

It's a treat to watch Manuel box. He is fast, smart, technically skilled, and very aggressive, which is odd, because outside the ring he is a quiet, sweet young man. He is by far the best boxer on the team. Last Saturday night we watched him dominate another opponent. He has attracted a lot of attention, and they have been taking him for weeks at a time to Mexicali for advanced training. The next step for him will involve trips to mainland Mexico, Cuba, and maybe Russia. Boxing is a passion for him, and is presenting him with opportunities that he would never otherwise have.

When Manuel fights he uses shoes that he shares with another fighter, has hand me down trunks and shirt, and shares headgear and gloves with several others. As I understand it, his next fight is a championship round, that if he wins, he may be on the Mexican Olympic boxing team. However, he will be required to have his own shoes, gloves and headgear. So it looks like we will be sponsoring a boxer, something I said I would never do. Oddly, I'm excited about it and hope this works out to be a dream come true, and a chance for Manuel to see the world.

# Juan

This is a story of love and ambition that, like Icarus, led a man too close to the flame, and it destroyed him.

The road from Mexicali to our little village is mostly straight for 120 miles. There is one spot, however, where the highway makes a few sharp turns through the hills, and one of the turns has a sharp drop off. That's where our story ends. Let's back up and see what led us there.

Juan was born in San Felipe and grew up without many creature comforts. His family scratched out a living fishing, and doing odd jobs in the off season. His parents both worked hard to raise the six children and although poor, they were fed. Their house was simple but clean. No heat or air conditioning not even electricity, and they had to buy 5 gallon bottles of water and carry them on their shoulders for drinking and cooking. Juan was born with an inherent entrepreneurial spirit, and was ambitious. He wanted to live like the rich people who had big houses and cars and dressed in colorful clothes. As he grew into his teen years he would walk down the street with a bucket of water and a rag and convince people to let him wash their cars for a few pesos. From that he saved enough money to rent a lot that had water, and he opened a real carwash. He did good work, washing, waxing and detailing cars. As his business increased, he started selling soft drinks to customers while they were waiting for their cars, then he added beer to the menu, and soon had a taco stand selling the best fish tacos in town. As his company grew he discovered that he could buy supplies cheaper in Mexicali, so he started taking the bus once a week and bringing back stock for his operations. By now he had several employees and he was happy, but still had growth plans.

Juan wasn't entirely consumed by work. He was a very handsome lad, and on Saturday night he would meet his friends on the Malecon to hang out, all dressed up in his new boots and cowboy shirt and jeans. Most of his friends just went there to drink cervesa, but Juan loved women. He was nicknamed Don Juan, and did his best to live up to the name, seducing several local ladies. Then his life took an abrupt change. He met Esperanza. He first saw her at a wedding. She was dressed in a colorful flowing skirt and a white blouse. She had long, black hair that flowed to the middle of her back, and beautiful eyebrows that blinked over eyes that you could get lost in. Juan was smitten. She became his obsession. He wooed her with all his charm. He would take her walking down the Malecon and along the beach on Saturday nights. He brought flowers, bought her burritos, and showered her with compliments, claiming his undying love.

Esperanza was an only child. Her parents were totally devoted to her, and had gone to great pains to raise her to be a good girl. They lived a modest life, her father was a waiter at a local tourist bar, and made pretty good tips during the tourist season. Her mother made empanadas, a small pastry filled with succulent meats or fruits. She would walk downtown and sell them on street corners. It wasn't much but it helped them to afford to send Esperanza to school, and although their house was small and had a dirt floor, they did have electricity. This made Esperanza even more desirable to Juan.

Juan was in full out frontal assault on Esperanza's virginity, but in spite of all his charm, she would not submit. When Juan tried to kiss her, she would modestly lower her head and look at her feet. She did let him put his arm around her as they strolled under the clear, starlit skies of night time San Felipe. The feel of her next to him was driving him wild. He even told her he loved her. That was a first for Juan. He had never gone that far with another woman, well except maybe in a moment of passion. Esperanza would smile demurely  and say, "I love you too mi amor, but I cannot do what you want until I'm married."

So it went every Saturday evening, Juan pursuing his conquest, Esperanza resisting, but just enough to keep him on the hook. Juan was an ambitious, driven man, but Esperanza was more than his equal when it came to the game of love. She had decided to marry him, and knew exactly what she needed to do to catch him. Of course, Juan was oblivious. He had no idea how well planned the strategy was, or how hopelessly lost he already was.

While Juan was chasing her on Saturdays, he was working hard during the week. By now his taco stand had grown into a full sized restaurant serving tacos, burritos, chiles relleno and a delicious variety of fish dishes served with rich sauces to delight local tastes. He was having trouble carrying all his supplies back on the bus every week. Juan needed a pickup truck. Consumer credit hasn't invaded our little village yet, so if you want a car you borrow what you can from your friends, and you buy an older used car. Juan did just that and bought an old ford pickup that had seen better days, but it ran, always a plus down here. The minimum driving age in Mexico is – well it's pretty vague and drivers ed doesn't exist. Driving is considered a sport, not an art. At any rate, Juan learned to drive through on the job training. Once a week he would drive to Mexicali, pick up supplies and drive back.

Now this is where the story starts to become a little more complicated. Let me try to tell it a piece at a time. We all know where the story is headed with Juan and Esperanza. Finally through a combination of frustration, lust and love, Juan proposed marriage. Esperanza lept into his arms, squealed, "Yes", and passionately kissed him on the lips. Juan thought he had just died and gone to heaven. They had a big wedding the following month, and the entire village came to witness the vows, and celebrate in true Mexican fashion until the following dawn. Juan was deliriously happy and the two lovers moved into a small casa rented from his cousin. Ten months later their first child, Juan Jr. was born. You could not ask for two more proud parents. Life was good. The business was growing, along with the baby, and within months Esperanza was pregnant again. As Esperanza became more focused on being a mother, and Juan became more focused on the growing business, they drifted into a comfortable, but a little boring routine. Juan was becoming restless.

With the growth of the business came to need for even more supplies from the city, so Juan was making the trip even more often. During one of the trips he went to buy chorizo for the restaurant and met Juanita. She worked the evening shift at the butcher shop that made the best chorizo this side of heaven. Juanita had just turned 18, and was a slim dark haired beauty, not at all unlike Esperanza. Juan and Juanita struck up a conversation, and Juan found himself staying later each trip, spending time with her before he drove back. As their relationship grew, the stress level on Juan also grew. He wanted to spend more time with her, but the long days and driving back in the middle of the night were wearing him out. After one particularly long day in the city, Juan complained to Juanita that he didn't look forward to driving all the way back that night and Juanita dropped the bomb. "Why don't you spend the night with me, and drive back in the morning?"

There was no rational thinking going on at that moment, by either one of them. Juan immediately accepted and his life was inalterably changed.

Juan started spending more time in Mexicali, and less time at home, frantically driving back and forth trying to keep two women happy and his business going. He was getting exhausted and started to become irritable, picking fights with his wife, snapping at employees, and making excuses to spend more time in the city. One Friday night Juan met his cousins downtown, and they started drinking together. It turned into a very late night, and a slightly drunk Juan decided he needed to see Juanita. So, at 3 AM, he headed North. He was driving fast and the old truck was dancing all over the highway. When Juan came to the curves in the mountains, he didn't make it. The truck crashed through the guard rail, over the embankment and came to rest at the bottom of the hill. Luckily he wasn't seriously hurt, but he was scared sober. Also luckily for him someone saw the accident, and they called for a wrecker to haul him out. Unfortunately, the truck was destroyed, and Juan was trapped inside.

That brings us back to where we started, the end of the story. I swear that it is true, as incredible as the ending really is. If this were fiction, no one would believe it. While they were waiting for the tow truck to arrive, a large refrigerated fish truck hauling freshly caught fish from the Sea of Cortez came up the highway. Just as it reached the curve a front tire blew out. The driver lost control, crashed through the guard rail and landed right on top of Juan. He never knew what hit him and was crushed to death immediately. That curve now has 13 crosses beside the road, memorializing all those who have lost their lives there, but for me Juan's cross will always touch me as we drive by, a little more carefully than before.

# A Dilemma

I have been stranded on the horns of a dilemma for the past couple of years. The problem centers around the issue of being worthless. It is something that I have learned a lot about over the last several years, and you might even say that I'm an expert. Being worthless is a lot different than doing nothing. Doing nothing is boring and depressing. Being worthless is an art form, not unlike becoming a concert pianist or a professional athlete. No one has ever been perfect at the arts or sports, and no one has ever perfected the art of becoming perfectly worthless. But that doesn't mean that we can't aspire to perfection, and achieve that state of mind that defies productive thought or action. Self denial plays a surprisingly large role in worthlessness. You need to deny the urge to have a productive job, be involved in community service or volunteer work. However, just like the recovering alcoholic, a practitioner of the art will occasionally do something worthwhile, just to proved that they can, without becoming totally enmeshed in positive actions.

A lot of basic management techniques are helpful to the student of worthlessness. Delegation being fairly high on the list. The credo, "Anything worth doing is worth delegating." Is worth committing to memory. The danger here is that the mere act of delegating could easily turn into something productive. The "delegate and disappear" operating plan might be more suited to those who have not been able to completely let go of the primal urge to accomplish something. Before rushing off to delegate something you should ask yourself, "is this something that really needs to be done at all?" As you become more proficient, you will discover that most things aren't worth doing, and the world doesn't change whether or not it gets done.

On the list of positive things involved in practicing the art are sunrises and sunsets. Sunrises are best taken with coffee, sunsets with gin. Relaxing with good friends and family is a core value of the professional. Other important activities are playing with dogs, siestas, contemplating life with no goal of learning anything, and siestas

I could go on for hours about all of the things that are important to this art, but I think you already have the point. Now back to the beginning. That's the dilemma we started talking about. I would love to give seminars on HOW TO BE WORTHLESS. As wired up as so many people are these days, this course could be a real lifesaver to the masses. They could change the world! The problem is that if I were to do that, I wouldn't be worthless. All the effort of the last few years would end up being wasted.

I guess the only option for me is to lead by example, and hope others can see the benefits of being really worthless.

Love from your worthless friend,

Sam

# *Snippets*

I love Mexico. The people are so kind, gentle and giving. They work very hard, but without the stress that is so much a part of life in the US. In some ways they are very modern, and in some pretty primitive. Just saw an example of the latter last week. We don't have a mechanized street sweeper here, and living in the desert, when we get a windstorm, the sand piles up everywhere. So what sweeping does happen is done by hand with pushbrooms. There was a crew last Friday sweeping up from the last blow. For safety they had one orange safety cone. It was in a wheelbarrow, behind them. There were no flaggers, or any other thing to protect them, just their faith that drivers would see them and move over. Their whole approach to traffic control is confounding to say the least.

The stop signs here in our little village fascinate me. We don't have any traffic lights, so stop signs are what sort of controls traffic. They are randomly placed throughout town, so you never know when is going to pop up. They are often hidden behind a palm tree or bushes. It's not uncommon for a small dirt road to intersect one of our main thoroughfares, and the stop sign is on the main street, not the side one. You are expected to see and obey them, sort of. There are some unwritten rules. For example, if you come to a stop sign, and a woman arrives at the intersection shortly after you, she has the right of way. She doesn't look right or left, she just goes. It only takes a few close calls to figure this out, and once you do, it works just fine. They do have a system that requires a driver's license, but it's pretty flexible. If you are tall enough to look through the steering wheel, you can drive. You do have to wait several years before you can apply for a license, but in the meantime it's not uncommon to see children barely out of diapers driving down the street. Driver's education hasn't moved this far south yet, so U turns from the right lane are accepted practice and speed limits are only suggestions that are seldom used. Actually they are universally ignored. The thing that makes the whole system work is attitude. Mexicans are a very patient bunch, and are very seldom aggressive drivers. In eleven years here, I have never seen anyone be flipped off.

As most of you know Diane was very sick over the holidays. It was a little scary for a while. She has finally fully recovered, and is going full tilt again. All of our employees are Mexican, and are just like family. They would not have our office Christmas party until Diane was well, so we are having it next Saturday. Those things are important to them. They also make tortillas or tamales, and when they do, they always bring some to Diane. It is such a blessing to have employees that are so reliable, and such wonderful people.

We are so lucky to live where it never snows, the sun shines daily, the sea and the mountains frame our world and we're safe. We are isolated from the outside world, and that's a good thing.

Love all of you,

Sam

# Been Thinking

I've been thinking lately. Mostly about life and its joys and tragedies. Living in Mexico gives me a glimpse of a simpler, much less harried way of living. All the modern gadgets that we have to make us more efficient, often distort our view of what is important. Take, for example, the digital camera. I finally figured out that it doesn't do an accurate job of capturing reality. It distorts what it sees, and disturbs what we know deep inside is really the TRUTH. Horse piddle, some of you more skeptical ones may say. How can something so mechanical and technically perfect in every way distort anything? Before you turn away and dismiss me as some sort of whacked out crackpot, let me explain. Well, I may be a little crazy, but at times I do have these flashes of insight.

This revelation has come to me slowly over the last few years, and at first I had no idea. I too subscribed to the theory that a camera only reflected what it saw. But last week, the proof of the inaccuracies was forcefully brought home to me. At first I just thought it was the angle of the shot, perhaps just a broken zipper on the dress pants of life. But as I thought about it, the pattern began to emerge. All of the recent pictures had the same flaw.

Incidentally, and totally not related in any way to this discussion, recently women have been treating me as a father figure. That can only be ascribed to a friendly nature, not at all age related.

Back to our conversation. The flaw in these pictures is that they show me as a white haired old man, with jowls hanging down that make me look like an old hound dog. THAT ISN'T POSSIBLY ACCURATE. I am not that old or run down. In real life I am still reasonably good looking, not a movie star or anything like that, but still decent looking. The only rational explanation of this phenomenon has to be a lens distortion in the camera. We need to have a dialog with the Japanese, who design all these technology thingys, and tell them that they are making a big mistake by trying to sell a product that makes us look much worse than we really are. It is way past time for action. We should prepare a petition

and call our congressmen for action. Or maybe just resign
ourselves to it and have a gin and tonic.

# What a Great Day

Berkeley came to visit us today. She lives in Mexicali about 120 miles away. She brought her 3 dogs. When you add them to our two, it looks like a dog kennel here. She has a puppy, Rocky, who is about 6 months old. He's a sweet dog, and of course at that age full of energy. In our courtyard we have a good sized swimming pool. Over the pool is a bridge, mostly for decorative purposes. This afternoon Rocky in his clumsy puppy way, was chasing one of the other dogs, who ran over the bridge. Rocky ran at the bridge, leapt at it and missed and landed in the water. Initially Rocky had a very surprised look on his face, then he just started swimming. At the time there were three women in the courtyard. They all panicked and ran to the edge of the pool. With the smooth, vertical sides of the pool, there was no way the dog could climb out. To make his plight even more serious, the water is still way too cold for swimming, and none of the women wanted to jump in to his rescue, so they are doing primitive dances around the edge holding their arms out towards the dog as if he could magically leap into their embrace.

As Shakespeare once said, "All's well that ends well." They managed to coax the dog to the steps at the end of the pool, and he climbed out, none the worse for wear. He wet down one of the women pretty well when he shook himself off. Even though the temperature was about 80 degrees right then, they dashed off to find a towel to dry him off so that he wouldn't get cold. All the time he is just enjoying all the attention, and totally unconcerned about the whole event. You could almost see him saying, "I meant to do that."

Michael and Gail have a two year old grandson visiting with his parents here. This whole episode with the dog started me wondering what would happen if he jumped in. Would I be willing to jump into that cold water to pull him out? Hmmm. Tough decision. I really, really hope that I'm not actually faced with that decision. Hopefully there will be someone braver than me there when it happens, or maybe he'll turn out to be one of those precocious kids who instinctively knows how to swim and where to find the steps. These things always work out for the best, so let's just not worry about it.

Love y'all

Sam

# A Wandering Mind

It's a commonly held opinion among the gringo population here in
our little village that someone who packs up their belongings and
leaves family and friends, a lifetime of experience, familiar streets
and customs, a common language, and moves to a third world
country at the very least has to be a little off center. We're down
here surrounded by a strange language, odd and sometimes
primitive laws, by byzantine restrictions on foreigners, and few, if
any, family and friends. We do have a community that ranges
from people avoiding legal problems to downright crazy. Normal
is a whole different paradigm here. They run the gamut from rich
to dirt poor, honest to criminal, genius to downright stupid. The
one thing we do have in common is that no one is "average". It is
definitely cheaper to live here, but there is something deeper that
brings people here. Maybe it's a pioneering spirit, or basic
restlessness that brings them. It does seem that they have all had
interesting lives up North. They don't often come from
government jobs, or boring careers. They were business owners,
or at least very independent employees, excepting the lawbreakers
of course. It's also interesting that what you did in your past is
rarely discussed. That was another world, and doesn't relate to life
here.   A few of them are very unhappy and mean spirited. They
complain about everything and go out of their way to insult their
hosts, the Mexicans. Most of them, however, are very alive and
creative. We have a large population of talented musicians and
artists and a large group who see opportunity in every situation,
and bring a special vitality to life in Mexico. Only a few of them
are capable of seeing things like most other people would. These
are the people who put the fun in dysfunctional.

Even the landscape here is a study in strange contrasts. We have
barren mountains 10 miles or so to the west, then desert from there
to the Sea of Cortez. The desert is arid and dry. One inch of rain
in an entire year is unusual. Some years we have no rain at all.
This desert runs all the way to the beaches of the sea. So we have
a very large body of water, and very parched land. It is puzzling to
the rational mind to put these side by side, and even stranger to
realize that the water is poison to the plants. The salt in the

seawater kills even the hardiest of cactus plants. To complete this strange picture, there are huge underground rivers of fresh water flowing under the mountains from the Pacific storms that hit the western slopes of the mountains. These underground rivers never surface just running unseen into the sea. Somehow, all these contrasts blend together to make a unified whole that creates a healing, comforting world. It has to be this strange combination of eco systems that affects the minds and thoughts of its residents.

Let me offer myself as an example of how wacky our minds work here. Yesterday I was performing my usual morning ritual of watching the sunrise. Spring is the time of year for the highest and lowest tides of the year, and yesterday morning happened to be a low tide. When that happens, it exposes an outcropping of rocks that is submerged most of the time. They have a volcanic look to them, very rugged and black. Incidentally they also harbor a rather substantial hot springs. Anyway, I was watching the sunrise and looking at the beauty of those rocks. They spend most of their time babysitting the sea life that lives around and is protected by them. But today they are sitting out enjoying their rare opportunity to warm themselves in the desert sunshine. I could just see them flexing their rocky shoulders, shaking off the water and feeling warm and contented in their brief respite from their job as foster parents to the little creatures.

Yes, you're right. I should probably be locked up, but in our community here, to tell this story at one of our frequent cocktail parties wouldn't even raise an eyebrow. People here understand that being relaxed and taking time to reflect often leads the mind on flights of fancy that do defy logic, make no sense, but provide the thinker with a fresh look at our world.

Take time to have a fresh look at your world. It brings a fun flavor to your day.

# *Bats*

This is a true story that happened a long time ago, when the Princess and I were a lot younger. Why this story flashed across my mind this morning will forever be shrouded in mystery. It's odd and fascinating how our minds work, especially early in the morning, when the world is quiet, and the coffee smells so good. So, on with the story:

Long before we even considered moving to the island, we fell in love with it, and often rented places for a weekend, or for vacations. This particular time we rented a rustic cabin on the west side of the island. It was just beautiful. It was set amongst tall fir trees with the land sloping down to the Puget Sound. Facing west meant gorgeous sunsets, in a quiet idyllic setting. The cabin was quite roomy with a big living room, a good sized kitchen and a master bedroom with a large stone fireplace. All the appliances were old, but serviceable and we had all the conveniences such as water and power. Even with that the atmosphere being there was like moving back in time to a more gentle lifestyle. We, of course had chosen the bedroom with the fireplace for sleeping, even though it was summer and we didn't need a fire. On the first night there we had just gone to sleep when things started going crazy. I was awakened by something brushing my face. I opened my eyes to the sight of several bats flitting frantically around the room. We figured out later that they had come in through a crack in the roof next to the stone chimney.

At about the same time the Princess woke up and screamed, and it was immediately my job as the man in the house to protect her. Leaping into action, I jumped out of bed in my summer night wear (nekkid) to protect her from being eaten by rabid, monster bats. It was just like a scene from a horror movie. The Princess jumped up and headed for the spare bedroom. She slid the door shut. (It was a sliding, pocket door). Now that she was a little safer, the next task is to rid the house of the dozen or so bats that were now flying all over the house. I reasoned that since I had heard that bats operate on radar, it should be fairly easy to use a broom and herd them outside. I opened the doors and went to work. Picture this if you will, me running all over the house waving and upside down broom still stark naked. It is difficult to maintain any sense of dignity while doing that. I'm sure you've all heard the cliché "like herding cats". Well let me assure you that herding bats is even more difficult. The little bastards are incredibly quick, and don't take suggestions well. I did actually eventually hit one with the broom, and stunned him. I swept him out the door. After several hours of madly dashing all over the house, they finally tired of the game and left. By now it's about 3AM, and I am bushed, but it wasn't over yet.

I turned my attention back to the Princess. As I mentioned, she had slid the bedroom door shut. To keep the bats from breaking down the door, she had slid a big chest of drawers up against the door. When she slammed it into the door, it came off the track and was jammed shut. No amount of grunting and straining was going to release that door. So now she is trapped in the bedroom and claustrophobia is setting in. So I convinced her to open the bedroom window, and I crawled in through the opening, with only a few minor scrapes, nevertheless painful. Once in the bedroom I pulled the chest away from the door. Once she was no longer panicked, she didn't have enough strength to move it herself. After some swearing, and panting we got the door back on track, and she escaped her little prison. It was all over for her. She immediately went to bed in the spare room and fell asleep instantly. I on the other hand, was still pumped with adrenaline from all the excitement, and there was no way I was going to sleep. So I sat and read a novel until daylight.

Once again, a quiet, peaceful vacation had turned into a mini-adventure. That's the sort of thing that seems to follow the Princess wherever she goes, and that's only one of the reasons I love her.

# Her First Car

You can't live this long without accumulating some great memories. I have noticed that recently some of them are vanishing, and thought that I should capture them before dissolute living erases what's left. One of my most special recollections is buying our daughter her first car. So let's sit back together and enjoy reminiscing about the good old days:

She was, and is, a wonderful daughter. In spite of her parents she has grown into a stable, loving woman, endowed with a sharp and intelligent mind. It was not always so. During her high school years she could best be described as an underachiever. Some might even say she was a screw up, but not me. She has always been sweet, but in her teens just not interested in school. We limped along until her senior year, and graduation was going to be too close to call. So, about two months before graduation, I told her that if she did succeed, I would buy her a car. That seemed to do the trick, and she cruised to the finish line with no problems. Well, there was one problem. Finding just the right car.

So, on Saturday we went used car shopping. I will never forget that day. We spent the entire day going from one car lot to another. We only saw a couple of cars that might work. The one I thought might be OK for her, she didn't like, and what she wanted wasn't something I was willing to buy. At the end of the day we both felt unclean, dealing with some of the seediest characters in town, trying to peddle some piece of junk on us. We were both depressed. We were no closer to finding a car than when we started.

The following night, our son was glancing through the want ads and said, "Dad, here is Julie's car." I have no idea how he knew, but he was dead on. It was for sale by owner, who lived in a run down trailer park. We went to see the car, and it was a cute little yellow Datsun. It was in great shape, and both of us loved it. I wrote a check to the owner, who was a big, burly, blue collar, somewhat intimidating hulk of a man. He had the car parked in a lean to that he had built attached to his trailer. I asked him if we could leave the car there for another week, until she actually graduated, and until we had it insured.

He said, "No problem. Would you just move it to the other side of my trailer, so I can use the carport?"

I said, "Sure, Here Julie are the keys to your new car. Would you do the honors, and move the car?"

Julie didn't say a word. She just took the keys, and climbed into the car. Now she wasn't even going out to the street. She just had to back the car out of the shed, across the lawn, and to the other side. She fastened her seatbelt, looked both ways over her shoulders, just like in driver's ed. She carefully put the car in gear to back out and turned the wheel. When she did that the left front corner of the car caught the corner post of the garage, and the whole structure collapsed onto the hood of the car. A huge cloud of dust erupted, honest to god, in a mushroom cloud. The look of terror and shock on her face was priceless! That was well over twenty years ago, and I still remember her face vividly.

For some reason this all struck me funny. I was literally doubled over with laughter, I could not even stand up straight. While this hysterical laughing was pouring out, I remember thinking that this guy is going to punch me out. While still laughing, I tried to tell him not to worry, we would fix everything and pay for the damage.

He surprised me by saying, "Don't worry about it. My ex-wife did the same thing."

All's well that ends well, as they say in Shakespeare classes. A week later when we came to pick up the car, he had fixed his carport AND had replaced the broken headlight, and repaired and repainted the dented hood. The car was as good as new, and he wouldn't take any money for it.

That car served her well for several years and It will always be one of my fondest memories.

# Boxing – Part 2

A few of you may remember that over a year ago I wrote a piece about Manuel, the teenage boxer. Since then he has continued to work hard, winning the title for Northern Baja, then for all of Baja, and for the last two weeks he has been down at Yucatan and he won the gold medal, making him the amateur boxing champion for all of Mexico. This trip was his first time on an airplane and first time traveling outside Baja. This has been an amazing opportunity for a young man from a family of modest means. For his trip we gave him about $15.00 for spending money. He used it to buy necklaces for his mother and my wife.

His championship fight was against an opponent who grossly outweighed him and was much taller. Manuel had to reach up to hit him. He still won! He is now a local celebrity with pictures of him with the mayor, interviews and is being swamped by well wishes from all their friends here in our little village. Just in case you didn't read the first article about him, the kids wear this big fluffy headgear, huge padded gloves and mouthpieces, and the fights are very carefully monitored. It is enough to mollify my aversion to violence.

It's almost breathtaking, all the attention being given this shy, sweet young man. This December he will be going to Cuba for a month to fight there. The boxing federation also wanted to take him to Mexico City for a year of intense training. His mother, wisely said no to that. She felt that the temptations for a 16 year old living alone in a big city would not be good for him. So instead of that, they are bringing a top ranked professional boxer here to help him train. I don't follow boxing, so his name didn't mean anything to me, but people who know about that sort of thing say that he is famous. All in all, it's a fairy tale story. Remember the name, Manuel Garcia.

# *Old*

Well, I guess it happens to all of us. It creeps up when we're not looking and when we realize what's happening, it's too late. Generally speaking, getting old isn't all that bad. It comes on so gradually that we become accustomed to the hair that slowly turns white, the belly that becomes rounder, the heavy breathing at the top of the stairs, the aches and pains that gradually appear so that we can learn to ignore them. Anyone who is over 50 can add to this list ad nauseam. Under the harsh light of reality we can see the symptoms, but most of us, me too, ignore and deny all the signs. We still see ourselves as middle aged at the worst, and even younger after a gin and tonic. We harbor these illusions that we can still play football and baseball and all kinds of active sports, if we really wanted to that is. Many of us still harbor the illusion that we are attractive to the opposite sex. Incidentally, this causes some highly amusing and often pathetic scenes, especially in cocktail lounges, where the illusion is reinforced by liquid courage. Denial is the key to enjoying old age. As long as we can cherish and believe what the mirror and our driver's license pictures are trying to tell us is a freaky distortion, we're just fine.

It all started yesterday quite innocently. It was the hottest day of the year, so far. So in the afternoon I went to the swimming pool to cool off and relax. After a nice swim, and doing several laps just to prove what good shape I'm in, I climbed out of the pool and let the breeze cool and dry me. It was just perfect! Then I happened to look at my chest. Talk about being shocked! It was just like being bonked on the head in an old Abbot and Costello movie. The hair on my boobs, which have grown almost to the point of needing a bra, had turned white! It must have just happened overnight. Completely WHITE! There was also a 2" square section of white hair next to my belly button, while all the hair surrounding it remained brown. The white hair stuck out like a lighthouse beacon. It was a horrible aha moment.

My denial system folded like a cheap tent. I saw the soft belly, all the white hair, the spindly arms and legs, and more facial wrinkles than an old hound dog. I started remembering all the times recently when I would walk into a room, and forget why I was there. Then there is the issue of people's names. So far, I haven't forgotten my wife's name, beyond that it's a crap shoot. All of the jokes about old people just came true.

I guess that the good news, if there is any, is that knowing I'm old will help me accept things as they are. It's ok to order from the senior menu, because that is enough food to fill you up. It's ok to accept all those senior discounts, and even read the AARP letters that come in the mail. It's ok to realize that you really do need a siesta in the afternoon, and going to bed at 9PM is also normal for old people. It is comforting to know that I'm not young and struggling to make a living, but retired and enjoying life. It ain't much but it's all I have to cling to.

Love ya'll

Sam

# A Day at Home

What a great day! Spent the entire afternoon at home. This morning we went to the Tuesday vegetable market to buy our fresh produce for the week. It's grown in real dirt without hormones or estrogen or testosterone, or any of that other stuff that makes cucumbers bigger than most men. I suspect that the primitive growing conditions here are at least partly responsible for us being so healthy at such an advanced age. All of this has nothing to do with what I sat down to tell you. Today was only fairly hot, about 100 degrees, and only fairly humid. There has been a nice breeze blowing off the Sea of Cortez. Perfect weather for flying. All of the neighborhood birds took the afternoon off. I don't know whether they were using vacation time or sick leave, but it was definitely their day to goof off. They had to be taking the day off because they were all too young and athletic to be retired. Well not really goof off. The pigeons were practicing close order formation flying, much like the Blue Angels, but much more complex and intricate. There was a whole flock of them swooping and diving around in the sky over our house, flying inches apart and never colliding, with rapid direction changes that had me standing on the deck with my mouth open. They dart around with an elaborate choreography that only they understand. It takes and incredible amount of coordination and planning to execute something like that, and they just do it on the spur of the moment, just for fun and beautifully. Then the pelicans join in the chorus hanging midair, floating in the wind, not moving their wings, just letting the air currents do all the work. These large clumsy birds are so graceful in the air, you just can't tire of watching them. There is airspace control more complex than any international airport.. The pelicans flying higher than the pigeons. I wonder if they appreciate the show below them? Then a pair of hummingbirds flew right in front of my face and starting dancing a ballet, beak to beak, belly to belly. (Remember that old Kingston Trio song, "Back to back, Belly to Belly'? If you're too young to know who they are, call me and I'll give you a synopsis of the song. The hummingbirds were nose to nose, eye to eye, holding perfectly motionless in the air. Then like someone fired the starting gun, they dashed off, probably to Panama at the rate they were flying. The seagulls were a little slow on the uptake, but they finally sent a flock to represent them at the show. They did a beautiful, gliding circling show that although slower than the pigeons, still conveyed a sense of the beauty of the day. And down on the ground the LBJ's (Little Brown Jobs), maybe sparrows to you birdwatchers, were hopping around pecking at little tiny things in the courtyard that even the most conscientious worker wouldn't notice. They don't walk, they have this cute little hop thing that they do that is half hop, half bounce. Wouldn't it be great to be able to do that?

As if that wasn't enough, we just had our stereo moved up to the living room from the bedroom. It had been down there for two years, and it isn't much fun to listen to music when you're asleep. So we never used it. We spent the afternoon listening to Bluegrass, Dolly Parton, Jazz trumpet and Pavarotti. Listening to Pavarotti in surround sound is dazzling. Our dogs even perked up their ears and tilted their head back and forth listening to him. They ignored the Bluegrass. Oh well, they're dogs and have very limited tastes. Watching performances like this, it is very difficult to worry about anything. All you can do is enjoy the moment. The perfect way to live.

Love the moment

Sam

# It Isn't Funny

We've all read about the importance of humor. Good health requires it. But, I guess that's just like exercising and eating a healthy diet. Only a few people actually do it and we all know that people who exercise and eat health food are weird. They are pompous, boring, self righteous asses, who die young. Nutritionists keep changing their ideas of what is healthy. Remember how salt was once bad, and how about butter? I'm sure that any day now we will start reading about the toxicity of granola and yoghurt. I'll go out on a limb here and give you a peek at a visit to the doctor in about 10 years:

Patient, " Doc, I don't know what's wrong, but I feel run down all the time."

Doctor, "Well, you lab results are in, and I can see why. You need to change your lifestyle. You aren't eating properly. I am going to prescribe for you a diet that will solve your problem, but only if you follow it faithfully. Here is what you need to do:

1. Eat at least one serving of mashed potatoes and gravy every day

2. Have chicken fried steak on Fridays

3. Chocolate cake is essential for a balanced breakfast. That's the most important meal of the day. You can occasionally substitute key lime pie if you like.

4. If you must, limit your intake of fruits and vegetables to once a week.

5. Any seafood you eat needs to be deep fried. The same goes for chicken.

6. When you go out to eat, go to McDonald's.

7. We've found that patients who drink more alcohol are more likely to be successful with this diet.

8. Smoking, both before and after eating also helps reduce cravings

Sorry, I got sidetracked. We were talking about humor. It's hard to find. Next time you're at an airport, look through the bookstore for a funny book. Good luck! Everything there is either self improvement, murder and mayhem, or in the better airports they do have some porn. In just about any setting look around to see how many people are laughing. If you do see that, you'll see a crowd around the person having the good time. We can all develop a sense of humor. Here are some exercises to try:

1. When someone flips you off on the freeway, blow them a kiss.

2. When you rear end someone, tell them not to be so anal.

3. When someone is threatening violence, ask to be last.

4. Find something to laugh about in everything you do.

5. Follow a laugh with feelings of happiness and joy

Just ignore this letter. I wasn't serious anyway.

## The Truth About Clouds

People with scientific minds, that is left or right brained, I can't
remember which is the "rational" side, give us an explanation of
the clouds that says that they are merely small drops of water
suspended in the sky. That is obviously patently untrue to the
critical mind. Examine these simple facts:

1.   Water is heavier than air

2.   Ergo (I've always wanted to use this word, but have never,
until now, had the opportunity) If clouds are small drops of water
they would fall out of the sky before even forming.

Therefore there has to be another explanation for their existence. I
have one. To follow this you will have to, as the saying goes, be
willing to temporarily suspend your disbelief. My opinion comes
from the other side of the brain. That would be the side that is
intuitive and creative. The details are very complex and
sometimes difficult to understand so be patient and only maybe it
will make sense at the end. That is the only rational explanation
for what follows;

Clouds are camouflage. There are little alien beings behind them.
They are known by a wide variety of names, angels, gnomes,
fairies, trolls, devils, (you can add your list of names here.) The
clouds are the place that they can rest during the day, and guide our
lives without being seen. It's kind of like the student lounge at a
large university. They hang out, do a little homework, tell stories
about how they have changed people's lives and plan future
mischief or blessings, depending on their characters. My theory is
that they focus mostly on individuals. They do influence global
events, but only through their control over individuals, not
nations. I must emphasize that this point is only conjecture,
because we just can't know everything, but so many world events
are disastrous, that can only be ascribed to human failures, not the
work of angels.

These beings, for lack of a better word come from other
dimensions that are beyond our usual 3D view. Modern science is

just starting to discover and explore these dimensions, and as they learn more it will dramatically change our view of the complexity or our world. Their origins are from a huge, unknown space, that bears little resemblance to our "concrete" world.

These creatures are very sensitive about being seen. When you are totally relaxed you might get a glimpse, or feel their presence, but that's the best we can hope for. They do have some human characteristics, but some very key differences. They are either good or bad, black or white. It's never in between with them. The good ones fill our lives with joy, the bad ones make everything we touch turn to poop. Just before dawn about once a month they have a meeting and divide up all the people on earth. It's the luck of the draw whether or not you get a good one or a bad one for the month. That explains why some days you get chicken and some days you get feathers. There are also months when two or more will compete for you. Those are the totally wild periods that take your breath away and wear you out. Those are the days that can leave you confused and bewildered about what just happened to you.

What, you might ask about those days when there are no clouds? How can they hide and still do their work? Glad you asked. They have the ability to blow about with the breeze, or live in the trees, or in the water. Their existence is much more flexible than anything we can imagine. That does make it more difficult for them to interfere with our lives, but it does give them great mobility. That explains why on breezy, cloudless days, life seems to move slower, and fewer big events occur in our lives. They only create the clouds when they need to regroup, and plan their master strategy for the coming moon cycle, or whatever cycle they use. I'm not real sure on this point, it's just an educated guess.

I can, however give you a picture of how their process works. They relax in the soft contours of the clouds, and place bets with each other. Something like, "I'll bet I can turn Ramon's world upside down by noon tomorrow." The response usually being along the lines of:

"I've seen your pathetic attempts to influence those miscreants down there, and you couldn't upset a glass of water, let alone a human."

"Ha! That shows how little you have seen. You should see me when I get serious. I'll bet you a pineapple smoothie I can do it."

"If you're serious about it, let's raise the bet. How about a smoothie, a backrub, a white light bath and immortality?"

"OK, big mouth, you're on. By noon tomorrow right?"

If you can imagine this scene being repeated an infinite number of times in less than a nanosecond, you have the picture.

Now on the surface, this discourse would seem to contradict everything that we have been taught about religion and God. That's not really the case. Just as the Church has traditionally opposed new thoughts or theories that break new ground, like admitting that the earth was not the center of the universe, this acknowledgement of the existence of unearthly spirits does nothing to damage the basic premise of a God who created the universe. These beings are merely a part of that creation. They do not diminish the omnipotence of a creator. It only adds to the wonder of the incredible power of the creation. It does not threaten the wages and retirement benefits of our church leaders. It actually strengthen the belief in the existence of our spiritual sides.

So, if we accept this totally insane document as having a kernel of validity, what does it change? What can we do about it? Who even cares? Once again, glad you asked. There is a lot we can do. For centuries the Catholic church has done exorcisms to rid people of the evil side of these demons, and often it works. By actively relating to them we can share in their work on our behalf. By acknowledging them, and being aware of them we can develop a relationship that enriches our lives. We can choose which of them to let into our lives, and which ones to reject. The method for doing this is remarkably simple.

If you take time every day to lie on your back, let your mind float and watch the clouds you can sometimes influence the outcome of the bets these beings are making on your life. Just the act of relaxing and letting your mind be open gives you access to their involvement in your life, and you can feel the "peace that passes all understanding". It's a foolproof plan, and you will find that if you do it, life will be more enjoyable at the least, and maybe even more exciting.

Keep on dreaming

Sam

# *Extreme Sports for Flies*

Event promoters would have us believe that they invented these fantastic extreme sports shows on TV, where people, most young, mentally challenged men go flying through the air on motorcycles, skateboards, snowboards, cars, trucks, parachutes, no parachutes, surfboards, sleds, and other vehicles not intended for the purpose. You can also see earlier versions of the same thing at rodeos, and just about any event involving horses. Most of the time the contestants end up in a crumpled heap, with only 5 or 6 bones in their bodies not broken and a concussion or even brain damage. In most instances one can make the argument that the brain damage occurred sometime before they tried the stunt. It's dramatic footage, and they replay the crashes ad nauseum. Personally, I don't like watching people hurt themselves, but I obviously don't understand, because they are quite popular and people spend a lot of money just to prepare for and go to these shows. That isn't what this story is about. This is the tale of the original extreme sports addicts, the flies.

Being retired gives a person time to observe and explore the world around us. That's me, and since the golf course is closed for repairs, there is way too much time for that. But, I digress. What has attracted my attention lately is the behavior of flies, and it is remarkably like that of humans. Most of them avoid people, and just go about their lives. They eat crap and garbage, then go home to the wife and breed. It's a pretty good life, and fairly safe. However there is a small percentage of them (Probably about 1%) who were just born to take risks, and they sign up for the extreme sport circuit. Quantitative data is a little scarce, but is appears obvious that they go through rigorous training for this life. They are like a cross between bullfighters and kung fu masters. Even with the training though, there is still a high mortality rate among them. Let me describe what they endure.

The essence of this life is to taunt humans. The training regimen consists of a lot of physical training, much like the Navy Seals. They learn to jump forward, backward, sideways, and for advanced sport they learn to jump sideways and downward over the edge of a table or counter. But I'm getting a little ahead of myself here. Let's follow the career development of one of these little bastards. (Notice I used the masculine gender. I'm not sure they all are males, but intuitively you would think so, because not many women are this stupid.)The first step is amateur taunting. You can recognize these beginners easily. They are the ones who lightly land in your hair and lightly tickle you. About all you can do is brush them off. By repeating the process they can irritate you and make your brushing more aggressive, but you can't really hurt them. As they progress they move to your arms, and finally your face. A more advanced move is to land directly in your food. No one is going to swat a fly in their food. The risk of death or bodily injury is very low at this level. You can also identify these flies by picking up a flyswatter. They are the ones who flee before you can even strike. The better trained ones play a more dangerous game.

They start with the usual taunting maneuvers to get your attention and to irritate you. Again, this is like a bullfight, only us humans are the hapless animals. Then they land on the table in front of you. When you pick up the swatter, they ignore you. Then when you use most of your large muscles to go in for the kill, they wait until the last nanosecond and leap out of the way. The ultimate maneuver is to go sideways and down so that they disappear, and leave you thinking that you got them. The next step is pure poetry. They hide for a few minutes, then reappear and land on your nose. That's the fly version of giving you the finger. Sometimes, I'm sure you've noticed, they travel in gangs. When they descend on your meal it can be overwhelming. You have everything from beginners on their first taunt, to experienced professionals doing impossible stunts to stay alive. When this happens, all we can do is grin and bear it. Just brush enough of them away to get at your dinner, and eat fast.

I hope that this treatise has given you some insight, and that in the future you can appreciate what these little insects are doing to entertain themselves. You can keep on swatting, but you're outnumbered.

# More Flies

My recent story about flies elicited some responses that were more interesting and thoughtful than the original effort. These responses are worth sharing, and they need some further clarification:

**Lake wrote: Since you have spent so much time studying flies can you tell me how they land on the ceiling? Back flip, belly roll, somersault? The flies appear to be flying along feet down, wings up and the next thing you know, they are upside down on the ceiling? How did they make the final approach?**

Well Lake, the answer is fairly straightforward. The flies that you see doing this are the elite corps of the extreme sport flies. They have gone way beyond the Navy Seal level training. They are graduates of the fly-Kung Fu school of mind control. They are taught by a grasshopper, incidentally the same one referred to in the Fung Fu movies. (You may have noticed that even average grasshoppers can land on a vertical surface.) This training is not focused on the physical aspect of the art, but on the power of the mind. The flies are put into a totally dark room then asked to fly around and let their minds float freely. Not many of the flies pass this test, but what it does is to train them to think upside down. Once they master that, landing on a ceiling is a no brainer.

**Darryl wrote: Sam I also did a small study of these little bastards. One of my observations is that in the more advanced (Navy Seal trained big bxxxxs) is that nanoseconds when our sagging muscles have flexed to their max, the ones that have got away have been trained in a more advanced school, but I am on to their little secret. They fly backwards away from the slowly moving fly swatter (because our sagging flexed muscles are not as fast as they once were.) So if you swat slightly behind the little bxxxxx your success rate will go up significantly.. Try it. You will be amazed!**

Thank you Darryl for sharing. I am impressed with your optimism. I do fear, however, that you are deluded in thinking that this will make a difference. There are too many of them, and they are too smart for us mere mortals. Finally there is the insight from Susie

**Susie wrote: Take another look at the picture of the fly. Did you see the size of those eyes? They are huge and can see everything in all directions. We don't stand a chance.**

Ah Susie. You do understand. The fly's eye is like a fisheye camera giving them a huge field of vision. They are watching you every single minute of every day. There is no place to hide. They are out to get us. It is a real nightmare out of a horror movie. We don't need to fear Hitchcock's Birds. It's the flies that are out to get us and they keep multiplying. I must admit though, that I feel so much better since I gave up hope.

Thanks to all of you who commented on the story. The feedback thrills me. The downside is that it encourages me to write more.

If you have questions or comments of any nature, let me know and we will try to explain the mysteries of life in future tales.

Love y'all

Sam

# *Yuk*

Just yesterday I was sitting in the courtyard relaxing and reading a book. It was way too late in the day to drink coffee, so I was enjoying the healing waters of a gin and tonic. The weather was perfect and relaxation was the goal. My quiet solitude was suddenly interrupted when a flock of seagulls flew over. That is no big deal. It happens all the time. However, this time, one of them pooped right on my head. My first reaction was to rush into the house and get some toilet paper, but I realized that by the time I was back outside, the bird would be over a mile away. After a good hairwashing, and another gin, I began to reflect on the whole incident. It occurred to me that the remarkable thing about it was that it doesn't happen more often than it does. Here we are, up to our ears in birds from the little hummingbirds that roost in our palm trees to the pelicans that glide overhead in large formations. In between are the sparrows, wrens, buzzards, seagulls and a host of other birds for whom I have no names. That's a lot of assholes pointed right at us. It would not be unreasonable to estimate that we would be hit at least once a month, if not more often.

One possible explanation is that they have good control over their expulsions, and have the consideration to wait until they are over an unpopulated area before letting go. The only reason we would be hit is that one of them has eaten something really rotten and is suffering from intestinal distress. That does seem a little unlikely.

Another explanation is that birds have not had a good experience with humans over the years. We have hunted them, poisoned them, destroyed their habitat with our factories, homes, and dams. We have trapped them, eaten some of them and generally made their lives miserable. Maybe, just maybe, when they see humans their anal sphincters just tighten up and we sit below unscathed.

Admittedly I don't really have a good answer, but I do know that from now on I will be wearing my big Mexican sombrero.

# Yoga

Here I am, 71 years old and just starting my first yoga class. It seems to be a girl thing. I'm the only male in the class. That in itself made me wonder what I've done to myself this time. The instructor, also female, started off reassuringly, telling us not to push ourselves too far. She said that if you need to rest, just assume the Child position. In that form you lie on your face, pull your knees up to your chest and rest your bottom on your heels. You then rotate you feet 180 degrees and tickle your butt. I have never tried relaxing that caused that much pain. After about 30 minutes of incredible body contortions I invented a new yoga position. You lie face down, spread eagled, and just try not to throw up. This position is called the Sammy.

Toward the end of the class we were being taught to assume the tree position. For the uninitiated this position involves standing on one foot and slowly pulling your other foot up to your crotch with the knee pointed outward to the side. Then you gradually swing your arms out and up until your hands meet directly over your head. Now you close your eyes and feel the white energy flowing through your body and you connect with the universe. You feel your inner sun moving from your pelvis to your rib cage. For beginners this is easy because the torn muscles give you that same burning sensation. Then you lift the foot you were standing on until your leg is parallel to the ground. You then hang like that midair for 5 minutes while praying for world peace and lasagna for dinner. Our guide told us that if we were a little unstable during this we could reach out and touch a wall for support. My bride, commonly known as the Princess, reached out to touch a wall, but touched a door instead. The door opened and she fell out of the room. It was like a Laurel and Hardy gag. Now some of the women in the class are world class serious about their practice, but when they saw the Princess fall out of the room they got what the Princess calls the church giggles. In just a heartbeat world peace was forgotten, and inner focus destroyed.

It couldn't have happened at a better time. I assumed the Sammy and gasped for air.

# Sam Grubb, OM

I've always been someone who liked to be in the background. My favorite times were when I was able to coach or teach someone to be successful, and watch them receive public recognition for their efforts. Being on stage is no fun at all, and is draining. Musicians love performing, and God bless them for that. I would rather have a root canal. But that is all changing. Two months ago Kat convinced me to let her publish some of my stories. I was reluctant to do that because they were just written for family and friends, and not intended to be seen by strangers. It can be embarrassing to expose yourself to the public, after all I am foremost a local businessman reflecting the conservative tastes that usually bore and irritate people. Now people are seeing a crazy, unbalanced old fool writing about insane things with stories that usually have no purpose, other than to be a little off center. (OK maybe a lot off center.)

At roughly the same time, I recorded a CD of some songs that I wrote that are no more intellectually challenging than the stories. That was done to mollify my children, who wanted them recorded before I died. That isn't the only thing they are eager about. They are convinced that I have bags of money hidden, and they want that too. They are way too eager for me to drop dead, but I try not to dissuade them from their interest. They know if they want a piece of the action, they will have to be nice to me. So far it's working. They're going to be really pissed when it does happen and they realize that I've managed to spend all of it on profligate living. That is the cosmic joke that tickles me to death, figuratively speaking. Anyway, back to the CD. It took on a life of it's own and is now scattered all over town, once again diminishing my credibility as a captain of industry.

There is a point to all of this, and we're getting close to it. I have actually enjoyed the notoriety that comes with all of this. The comments from readers at Katskorner just tickle me no end. They are delightful, and some are wonderfully creative. I have become addicted to them. So, with this in mind, it has occurred to me that as a semi-famous author I need credentials to give legitimacy to my ramblings and opinions. I never made it to medical school, law school, vet. School, or accounting school. You could write books about the things I don't know. It has occurred to me however, that just having initials after your name gives you an air of authority, even if no one has a clue what the initials are. Hell, even life insurance salespeople have initials after their names, or financial planners. So after only a couple of minutes of thought, I have decided to give myself initials after my name. From now on I will be Sam Grubb OM. Can you feel the difference? Here is a man of substance and wisdom who has achieved an advanced degree. No one can guess what, but with initials like that, it must be pretty special. OK, I'll tell. Just between you and me, the initials stand for Old Man. It is a title I have earned, and richly deserve. Let me know just how impressed you really are.

Respectfully yours,

Sam Grubb OM

## *Dolphins*

There is a fascination with the sunrise here on the Baja. The Sea
of Cortez is calm, and there are always some light morning clouds
on the horizon to give color to the morning show. It's a quiet time
of day and the sun puts on a light show that far exceeds the man
made light shows at concerts. This morning we had a special
bonus feature. I was drinking coffee on the deck, watching the sun
come up over the horizon, enjoying the quiet but spectacular
changing colors. There, swimming right up next to the shore in
front of our casa, was a pod of dolphins. They were leisurely
floating along doing their morning stretching exercises. They
would loop up out of the water, and gracefully slip back in. There
were probably 50 or so of them playing in the water as they did the
dolphin version of strolling by. Try to add all this up in your mind;
a beautiful, quiet morning, a shrimp boat offshore headed out with
his nets, and a pod of dolphins playing in the foreground. It's a
magical, healing scene. It brings a soft smile to your face, and a
feeling of tranquility to your soul.


Well, I gave it my best shot, but my words just can't capture the
magic. It's poetic and musical and touches the soul. I guess you
just have to be here to feel the gentle power of these mornings. On
a lighter note, I've been doing a little songwriting lately, and in a
moment of weakness went down and played at a bar. Two good
friends perform there on the weekends, doing acoustic folk music.
They have been playing together for several years now, and they're
very good. I played during their break. They've asked me to come
regularly to play with them. I turned them down, because playing
the other night reminded me how I just don't like playing in
public. Then they asked me if they could do some of my songs.
They promised not to change the words or the melodies. I told
them to go ahead, and to feel free to change anything they wanted.
It could only improve the songs. Looks like I'm on my way to
becoming a famous songwriter. Here is a first draft of my
acceptance speech at the Grammys, or one of those award thingys.

Thank you. The trophy is OK, but all the cool stuff that the sponsors gave me is really cool, except for the gold Rolex watch. I don't wear one, and don't really care what time it is. Maybe I'll sell it to some uptight ass who worries about that sort of thing. If you're interested, see me after the show. Oh, and by the way, I put some of that fancy designer bottled water in my goldfish bowl, and they died. A bottle of cheap gin would have been a lot more attractive to me. I will say that the hotel room is amazing. It's the first one I've ever been in that doesn't charge by the hour. Can you imagine that? They just expect that you'll stay all night. I wonder who stays in places like that for the rest of the year. The bathroom is bigger than most motel rooms I've seen and you should see the cars they bring you here in. I've lived in apartments smaller than those cars, and the champagne tickles my nose. Next year I'll just bring my own gin, thank you.

Oh, and I would like to also thank all the little people. It's the stupid things that you do that inspires me to write songs about you. I've seen enough of that here to give me material to write for the rest of my life. And finally, to my family and friends. For years you've all told me that my songs were dog poop. Well here I am, you're still in your miserable little lives back home, and ha, ha, ha. I got the last laugh. I have a lot more I'd like to say but there is a serious party as soon as this thing is over, Thank you, I'll see you up here next year.

# Golfers

Although golf can be played by people of all ages, most of them are older and retired men. They are men desperate to get out of the house. Their wives have explained to them that they are married for better or worse, but not for lunch. So golf is a natural choice. It's not too strenuous, takes most of the day, and is a good time for male bonding. When a newly retired guy takes up golf, it's fun to watch the progression from hacker to serious golfer. There seems to be an inbred progression in the development of a golfer that follows a rigid pattern.

The starting point usually seems to be a man who, if he drinks at all, drinks moderately. His language is normally quite clean, and his disposition is usually nice and polite. At first, though he plays horribly, he enjoys the game. Then one day he hits the perfect shot. The smooth feel, the beautiful flight of the ball, watching it land on the green are indeed special moments. Now he is hooked, and the personality change is dramatic, and to an outsider, shocking. He has experienced Nirvana, that perfect moment where the whole universe becomes perfect for just an instant. It is now an addiction as severe and debilitating as hard drugs. The problem is that he now expects every shot to be that perfect. If you've ever played you know that to have that happen once in every round is exceptionally lucky. So you are left with about 100 ugly shots and maybe, just maybe, one good one. Now, the man who used to be cheerful and fun to play with becomes an ass. He complains bitterly about every shot. All of a sudden the golf course is in terrible shape, the wind is unfair, and the sand in the bunkers is a mess, and on and on.

The standard solution to this problem is new clubs. After a couple of thousand dollars with no noticeable improvement, the new clubs are deemed to be defective. Never in this process is any thought given to taking lessons. Watching golf on TV, and taking advice from golfers who are worse than he is are the standard solutions. Practicing is not a viable solution either. Just grab the clubs and head out on the course, expecting that today is the day that it will all come together. A rational observer could see that no improvement is happening and that another approach is necessary. However, if he were a rational observer, he would not be playing this stupid game in the first place. The insanity of it all is that every time he heads out to the course, he expects to do better, and every time that doesn't happen. This can go on for years and he never stops to ask what is wrong with this picture. It is classic addictive behavior and it begins to show in his habits.

The first symptom is language. It deteriorates. A formerly polite man turns to the foulest words in the English language. The swearing permeates every sentence. This is not just casual cursing. This is violent swearing. The kind that embarrasses even sailors. "Whoa, where did that come from?" is the stunned response of old friends. The second symptom is drinking. I'm a good example of that. For 27 years I didn't have a single drink of any kind of alcohol. I retired, took up golf, and started drinking. I don't think that humans are capable of tolerating the stress of golf without drinking, at a minimum after the round, and on some days, even during the round. This, of course, does nothing to improve the quality of the game, and just increases the frustration level. But nothing rational is occurring here. There is just something about the game that disables any logical thinking parts of the brain.

So now we have a golfer. A foul-mouthed, drunk, who still believes that the next time he plays it will be better. And it never is.

# Bubba

Some of you probably know Bubba. He moved here to our little village several years ago from Fly Carcass, Kentucky. His reason for moving here is shrouded in mystery, but there are hints that the move wasn't entirely voluntary. Those of us who do know him realize that he is the consummate Redneck. Unlike the Kay jewelry commercial that says "Every kiss begins with Kay", Bubba is convinced that every kiss starts with a Bud Light, or for a serious conquest, box wine. His opinions cover a wide range of topics, and in his mind they are not just opinions, they are fact! At times he reminds me of Cliff from the TV series "Cheers". Bubba is a cesspool of worthless information, and is the world's leading expert. For example, he will find a way to interject into a conversation about breast reduction surgery the fact that the speed of light is 299,792,458 meters per second, and the circumference of the earth is 24,901.55 miles at the equator. He would never admit it, but he can't quite do the math to figure out how long it would take a beam to travel around the world. That question causes him to squirm, order more beer, and change the subject. This is usually the time that we learn that hummingbirds are carnivores. They only use nectar from flowers and feeders to power their search for insects. After warming up with little known facts, and beer, he can start on the world economic condition. If you let him ramp up to full speed, his ramblings can seem as long as the fourth grade. And pity the poor soul who has the temerity to interrupt or disagree with him.

That is not to say that Bubba doesn't have his redeeming qualities. He is quick to pick up a check at our staff meetings, following a golf game. He is a soft touch to anyone who is broke, and is first in line to go out of his way to help anyone who is in trouble. His heart is every bit as big as his mouth.

Bubba just seems to career from one disaster to another and he loves telling about them. His retelling, however, often invokes the poetic license rule. The stories are embellished, and tend to minimize the fact that he really screwed that one up. His latest adventure involves a little boat that he saw sitting next to a little shack out in the desert. It was love at first sight, so he introduced himself to the owner, and bought it for $200. This boat had obviously been sitting there since before Mexican Independence. The fiberglass was cracked, and the engine should have been in a Mercury outboard museum, and the upholstery was just a few shreds of faded vinyl. Bubba was just bursting with pride at his new fishin' boat. Obviously the first step was to restore the boat to working order, so Bubba enlisted Pancho to help.

Now Pancho is an old fashioned Mexican mechanic. He is truly gifted at the temporary fix. He has endured a lifetime of not having the proper tools or repair parts, but he can make anything run, for a little while. So they put some air in the trailer tires and headed straight to the water. They made it almost to the launch ramp before the bearings froze up, but they just dragged it the rest of the way. They met Leroy, whose job it was to get beer and bait, in that order. Immediately the boat went in the water, and Pancho fired it up. It coughed, choked, sputtered, but then miraculously turned over and they headed out to sea.

This is the point where the story becomes scary, ugly and life threatening. It is a tribute to how stupid us humans can be. Things were going smoothly and the beer was cold in the big red cooler that Leroy had brought. Once out in the middle of the bay they stopped to bait up and start fishing. That is when things went horribly wrong. As long as the boat was up on a plane, everything was just fine. When they stopped the boat started sinking. It had not occurred to them to put the drain plug in. Nor had is occurred to Bubba to put life jackets, flares, or a bucket to bail onboard. They were so engrossed in baiting their hooks, that by the time they realized what was happening, it was way too late. Pancho, being the quick thinking one, grabbed the one lifejacket and slipped into the water. Luckily he was a tiny man, because the lifejacket was just about as old as the first water on earth. By slowly paddling around he had enough buoyancy to barely float. Things were a little more complicated for Bubba and Leroy. As the boat sank from under them, the cooler floated in front of them, and they grabbed it for flotation. Thinking fast, Bubba opened the cooler and helped himself to another beer. As he explained to

Leroy, if we're going to die, it would be a shame to leave behind cold beer. So now we have our three mariners floating helplessly about a mile offshore in a choppy sea. No other boats were in sight. In a word, they were screwed. Now, here comes the miracle part, which shouldn't surprise us, because that is what has kept Bubba alive for over 50 years.

After a little over two hours, and 4 beers a fishing boat returning with his day's catch came across them. Even though Bubba and Leroy had greatly impaired motor skills by this time, they were hauled aboard with much grunting and swearing. Bubba insisted on rescuing the cooler too, because it had more beer in it. After opening a round of beers, Leroy mumbled "Pancho"

"Who's Pancho" said the fisherman.

"Pancho" said Leroy. "He's floating"

He had drifted away from the cooler, so the boat made a slow circle, and luckily found Juan who was just semi-conscious. So the gaffed hooked his belt and clumsily hauled him aboard . They bruised the entire right side of his body hauling him up the side of the boat, and rolled him into the dead fish in the bottom of the boat. When Pancho got home that night, all bruised up and smelling life fish, his wife said, "I don't want to know. You've been out with Bubba again haven't you?"

Pancho and Leroy were seriously shaken by the event, and both have sworn they will never, ever get in a boat again. A smarter vow would be to avoid Bubba at all costs. Bubba seemed to enjoy it all, and is proud of the fact that they didn't lose a single beer in the accident.

This story doesn't have an end, yet. As long as Bubba is alive, there will be more to come.

# Mexican Art

You've all heard the cliché that "Art imitates life". I experienced that yesterday. I was in Ensenada with time to kill, so went to the art gallery. There was a black and white photo exhibit that featured pictures of average Mexicans. There were street vendors, welders, and construction workers of all sizes and shapes. It was an aha moment for me. The looks on all of their faces were priceless. You could see the pride and the independence and determination in all of them. None of them had food stamps, or welfare programs, which really don't exist here. But none of them expected that. They were surviving on their own. There was an underlying happiness and strength to them that is so different than in the States. There was no hint of victim, or someone should take care of me.

# Rainy Morning

We had a light sprinkle this morning about 5:30. It was just enough to dampen the ground, and give us a brief respite from the daily hand to hand combat that we fight here with the fine dust that creeps in through solid block walls and covers everything with a fine, tan coating. Here in our sleepy little village rain is a miracle that awakens the town to the freshness that only this heaven sent cleansing can give. For a while everything was perfectly quiet. The Sea of Cortez looks like a lake, perfectly flat and glassy smooth with one fishing boat offshore to give contrast to the scene. The morning breeze is on its coffee break and nothing is moving. What a perfect scene that brings peace and wonder to the mind, and an awe of the beauty and complexity of our world. As if on command, just like the quiet that surrounds a concert hall when the conductor raises his baton, the morning songbird flew in and landed right on the tip of a cactus skeleton, and began her morning aria, announcing to the world the new day, and touching our hearts with the passion of her song.

The healing power of these moments is amazing. I've been working on a new music CD for the past month or so. We've assembled a team of real professionals to help, and frankly I was becoming way too uptight about the whole thing, and the joy was gone. The time in the studio is brutally intense. Everything has to be just right, and for a casual musician like me it can become overwhelming. Then there is the photo shoot for the cover art, coordinating with the other musicians who will be singing with me, producing the discs etc. The complexity of the task has stunned me. It took the beautiful moments of this cleansing moments to restore a sense of balance. The whole point of this project was to have some fun, and learn about recording, and I am back to that point. My team is composed entirely of wonderful, caring people who are there only to make this thing work. They are giving their time and talents generously, and none of them are drinking too much during the sessions. However, I plan to give all of them the opportunity to do just that once we are finished.

I hope that everyone has one of those magical moments today that makes us appreciate just how precious and gorgeous our lives can be, if we only have a moment to see and feel the awe.

By the way, the title of the CD is "DISCOVERING THE FUN IN DYSFUNCTIONAL".

# Good Morning

This morning in the predawn light just before sunrise a huge flock of pelicans silently glided right over our courtyard. They were intent on going to their offices to type up reports on the weather, tide charts, fishing conditions and whatever else pelicans do when they work. They have it all figured out. They knock out the paperwork, then they spend most of the day either fishing or just floating around looking down looking down at the beautiful Sea of Cortez. You can just imagine the wonderful sights they must see. Pods of Vaquitas, a small dolphin species that lives here, and are a very endangered group. We hope they can survive. Even this far North they occasionally see huge whales, seals and small fish jumping. That is the signal for the pelicans to dive into the sea for lunch. When they dive it reminds you of a WWII dive bomber. They go straight in with their wings partially out and constantly moving slightly changing their angle of attack as they go in. At the instant of impact the wings extend fully in a braking action so that they can dive full out into less than a foot of water and not break their necks. The intricacy of this ballet is wonder inspiring.

Right behind the pelicans a pair of bats flew in to take a drink from our swimming pool. They fly around with their rapid darting style, and swoop down to just touch the surface of the water, then fly up for another loop at the pool. The sparrows and hummingbirds like to sleep in. We don't see them until after sunrise. The sparrows, and a series of other as yet unidentified birds arrive to hop around and pick up little stuff from the wide variety of plants we have. There are several date palms with green dates just starting to ripen, hanging in big bunches from high up. Some of the impatient birds will eat them green, and our dogs also eat the ones that fall on the ground. I wonder if the birds poop like the dogs do after eating green dates? Shortly after the little birds, the even smaller hummingbirds arrive, darting around drinking from the flowers, then at break time they settle into the palm trees to wait for the signal to go back to work. I have no idea what that signal is. I have never heard the hummingbird version of the factory whistle. But they do hear it, for all at once they all leap into action. Our plumera plant is blooming now. (That's the flower that the

Hawaiians us to make leis. It's very fragrant), and the oleanders, and assorted other plants give them a daily feast of nectar. But I'm getting ahead of myself here.

I had to take a little break in writing this to go watch the sunrise. There is a narrow bank of clouds on the horizon to the east that seems to be there almost every morning. Just before sunrise they turn a wide variety of oranges from pastel to bright. Suddenly the sun pops up for a minute, then hides behind the clouds for a few minutes, with a few bright yellow shafts of light bouncing through them. In short order the sun burns off those clouds, and we have the usual cloudless day coming to life. In these few moments it is as if the world stops to bless the new day and everything is totally quiet. It is always a magical moment. This morning the silence was broken by some children showing up on the beach. They are laughing, running up and down and playing in the gentle surf that is washing ashore as the morning tide begins to recede. This is the time I have to hold my little dog up so that she can see over the wall on our deck and look over her world. She smells the air for new scents and carefully examines the courtyard and the sea to make sure everything is in its rightful place. Holding her like that makes me love her even more. These are special moments.

I started this writing to describe our courtyard, and boy did I get sidetracked. It too is a thing of beauty. It's about 150 feet long with one half dominated by a swimming pool shaped roughly like a guitar and with a little bridge over the middle of it. The other half is a gorgeous garden of palm trees, oleander bushes, barrel cacti, and several other varieties. Then there are the flowers and bunches of grasses. It is truly a tranquil place. It is extremely difficult to be stressed out in this secluded place. We are truly blessed and thankful to live such a life of

Hope this finds you well, and don't forget to find some joy in today.

Love all of you

Sam

# CD

I'd like to use today's posting for some shameless self promotion.
**IT'S FINALLY DONE!!!** After two months of intense work the
new CD is ready for release. This project includes many of the
best musicians in San Felipe. Here's the list in no particular order:

Denny Flannigan – He has graciously allowed us to use his song,
"My Reward"

Jim Manning – Is singing harmony on "Marvelous Toy" and has
allowed us the use of his song, "Mandy"

Ken and Sue – Are singing with me on the gospel song, "Little
Mountain Church"

Marjorie Scott – Is singing beautiful harmony on "Jimmy Brown"

Tom O'Neill – has composed the melody and is singing my words
to "Baja Sunrise"

Marion Law – Is doing a great job of singing "Amazing Grace"
with me.

Hal Radisky – Has allowed us to use his song, "One Meatball"

Bill Cartwright has allowed me to use two of the songs he has
written. Thanks Bill for letting me butcher your work.

And last but least, there are a bunch of songs I've written or stolen.

Rick Rudd has done the art work

Terry Van Arsdale has done the photography

Derek Wille has done the recording, editing, mixing, and all those
other things that happen when sound engineers do this kind of
thing. I have no clue what he really does, but he can make passing
wind sound like the Los Angeles Philharmonic Orchestra. He has
also provided counseling services when this whole thing seemed
overwhelming.

All of these people have generously donated their time, support and enthusiasm to bring together what is a very entertaining hour of music.

# It's Beautiful

Last night there was a full moon. WOW! The sight of the moon peeking over the horizon to see if it's safe to come out, then rising into view with a bright orange color that is just radiant is miraculous to see. It was so bright that all the stars in the area turned off out of respect for the splendor of the show. The Sea of Cortez came to life, reflecting the glory of the show. As the moon rose it gradually turned to a pure yellow color, and intensified its magic glow. In response, the sea lit up, reflecting the power of the moon. Capturing with words the magnificence of this phenomenon just isn't possible. The feelings of awe and wonder that it engenders fills you with a reflected glow that is spellbinding.

As if that weren't enough, there was a sunrise this morning. I know that is not a breaking news story, but it too is testimony to the beauty that surrounds us daily. At first light there isn't much color, just a tentative hint of grey with a promise that it's going become better with age. Sure enough, as the sky lightens the pale pastels start to appear as both the sky and the sea begin to awaken. The sky leads the way as the hint of orange begins to lighten the horizon. Then slowly, ever so slowly, the colors become more intense as the morning does its morning stretching exercises. You can see the sun just under the horizon, waiting for its first curtain call, and the sea begins to move from pale grey toward the greens and blues of the new day. Finally the sun makes its grand entrance, rapidly clearing the horizon to take a look at what today will bring. The bright colors of the pre dawn show disappear, but the sea begins to come alive as the colors in the water intensify, and are accented by the white trail left by the fishing boats heading out to harvest some of the richness that makes living here so tasty.

Being surrounded by this staggering beauty can only reaffirm our faith that this is a good life, and if we carry that wonder with us through the day, it will enrich our lives and the lives of those around us. My mantra for today is, "Hot damn, I can hardly wait to see what happens today!"

# Mexico

Spanish speaking people say Meh – e – ko, as opposed to the English, Mexico. Basically the x in Mexico is silent. OK, you might say, 'so what?" Well it is that difference in pronunciation that caused the following adventure, or if you are a wife of one of the protagonists, a disaster.

It all started innocently enough, if anything involving Bubba can be innocent. We started the day trying to drink the "X" out of Mexico. We were doing pretty well when he convinced Leroy and me to go fishing with him. With his history of almost fatal mishaps on the water, we should have known better, but when the male bonding gene kicks in, smart decisions get lost in the enthusiasm. And, if nothing else, Bubba is very convincing. He is the world's leading expert. This day his expertise was focused on telling us how he could guarantee a boatload of fish, and be home before the wives realized that we had left. His glowing description combined with a greasy burrito and a few beers was all it took to turn us into real idiots. We headed for the launch ramp with visions of world record catches dancing before our somewhat blurry eyes.

There is an old cliché about how God watches over fools, or something like that. He was surely on our side today. We loaded poles, nets, coolers and a peanut butter sandwich that had been in Leroy's pocket for a day or two. Bubba backed his boat into the water and it floated off the trailer. Let me take a minute here to describe the boat. It was a 14 foot aluminum thing with an antique outboard. It was barely suitable for a small pond, let alone the Sea of Cortez. He was good at launching. The only problem was that the boat wasn't tied off to anything. When it hit the water and reached the flotation point, it kept going. Leroy was first to react.

He stood there on the dock and said, "Oh shit."

Bubba said, "Oh shit, not again."

Luckily the boat didn't go very far. It just settled down into the water. Bubba had forgotten to put the drain plug in it. By the time we figured out that we should jump in the water and drag it in, it was awash, then disappeared, leaving the beer cooler floating. That was the catalyst. All three of us jumped in to save the beer. After much thrashing coughing and choking, we dragged to cooler ashore, and sat there like drowned rats and did the only rational thing left. We started drinking.

If you've read other Bubba stories, you realize that nothing fazes him. He borrowed a cell phone, because ours were wet and ruined, and called a wrecker, then when the tow truck arrived,(bubba was on a first name basis with the driver) he hired a kid to take the cable from the truck and swim out to hook it to the boat. Then it was a simple matter for the driver to pull the boat onto the trailer. The hull was scraped and the interior was a mucky mess, other than that you wouldn't even notice that something had gone wrong. So $100 later, and an empty cooler, we decided to drop in to the Miramar.

What were we thinking, you might ask. Truthfully, I just can't answer that question. We were still wet and shaggy, and looked like we'd been thoroughly trashed. Fortunately, the Miramar is a casual place on a good day. On a normal day there are a delightful mixture of characters who defy any description that would include the word normal. Our appearance didn't even rate a second glance, or a "What the hell happened to you guys?" Bubba had already recovered, and was excitedly telling us what a great time that had been, and he started ordering shots of tequila. Normally the Miramar is a safe place, but not on this night. Someone blew the whistle on us. Just as our clothes were drying, and our noses were wet, our wives showed up. What an intimidating sight that is. Three women standing there in front of us with their arms crossed across their chests, feet planted, and staring at us with looks that were more intense than something from Starwars. "What in the world did I ever see in you?" "You could have been killed." "When are you going to grow up?"

We all know that there is no right answer to those questions. If any of you readers have any suggestions on what a husband can do in this situation, I would be eternally grateful if you would share it. I tried explaining that this was much better than them having to come bail us out of jail again. That didn't work. Also, if I ever go drinking with Bubba again, shoot me. Well, maybe a couple of beers with him would be alright.

Thanks

Sam

# Chickens

Yesterday I was driving down a dusty dirt road out in the Ehido (the Mexican equivalent of a reservation) when a chicken ran across the road, just in front of me. She was in a big hurry to go somewhere. She didn't just cross the road, she RAN across it. That started me thinking. (Yes, I know what's crossing your mind right now.) Why was that chicken in such a hurry? Where was she going? At this point all we can do is speculate. Perhaps it was feeding time at home, and she didn't want to miss it. She was a very scrawny bird, so food would be a big deal to her. Another possibility is that someone wanted chicken for dinner, and she didn't want to volunteer for that.

Perhaps, just perhaps, she had made a promise to her husband, then wandered off and forgot about it until the last minute. The last thing she wanted to deal with was an angry, frustrated rooster. You can just picture him, sitting there at home in his little chicken recliner, frowning and wondering where the hell his wife had wandered off to this time. This all happened mid-afternoon, so the rooster had started with the tequila shots about two hours ago and he was in no mood for foreplay. There were about half a dozen little chicks wandering around the neighborhood. Now I don't know for certain that they belonged to the couple we're talking about here, but the odds are they did. The father probably resented having to babysit them while the hen was off doing god knows what. His mood was worsening by the minute as he sat in his chair smoking his cigar, and saying, "Harrumph" every time one of the chicks peeped at him. If all this is true, she really did need to hurry home to distract him before the situation became ugly.

It's entirely possible that my imagination has spiraled out of control. She probably wasn't even engaged, let alone married. Maybe she was single, and was rushing off to a date with the new rooster in town. Out here in the desert the dating options are severely limited, and she didn't want that slut hen from downtown to beat her to him. It's also possible that she was just training to run a marathon. Can you imagine the publicity if a chicken won an Olympic gold medal? Now that I think about it, that may be the right answer. She had that skinny, haggard look that typifies long distance runners.

This appears to be one of those things that the more you think about it, the more confusing it becomes. As the list of possibilities streams through your head, the options become more convoluted and they multiply like flies at a picnic. It would ease my troubled mind a great deal if someone reading this could explain why the chicken crossed the road.

# No Joke

Life is no joke, but it is a funny story. In every situation there is something in retrospect that can amuse us. It's the small disasters at the wedding that make the ceremony memorable. On a larger scale the same rules apply. For example Ghandi is famous for his work for peace. He was a frail man who walked around in only a robe, barefoot and ate a very simple diet that undoubtedly gave him bad breath. It was probably something like brussel sprouts without cheese sauce. He can be summarized in a single word: a supercallusedfragilemysticwithhalitosis.

Life, both individually and globally, is a stew of love, hate, anger, joy, frustration, relief with the occasional heartache of psoriasis. New age gurus tell us that we choose which we live with and that we should choose joy. I say, cat droppings! There are days when anger chooses us. When the toilet backs up and overflows, I don't know anyone who can choose joy. "Look Martha, the toilet has overflowed. Aren't we blessed to be able to witness this miracle? Let's just let it be so we won't interrupt it's karma." In the meantime the whole house smells like shit, the carpet is ruined, and you have 30 people coming to dinner, including your boss. It is, however, an opportunity for the plumber to screw you out of $500 that you can ill afford right now because your pregnant teenaged daughter has just moved back into the house with her unemployed boyfriend who has multiple body piercings. All you can do at this point is go to work cleaning up the messes, or run away from home. At the time there is not a lot of joy in the air at your house. To deal with the frustrations, you need to solve the problems one at a time, and feel the frustration while you are doing it. Call the plumber, call the restoration contractor, castrate the boyfriend, etc. Then in retrospect you can see the humor, and experience the joy of having a good story to tell your friends.

So my friends, the moral of this story is: Feel the emotion, acknowledge it, then move through it, always pointing towards the joy of a good laugh.

# No Rest For the Wicked

What a wonderful morning. The sun came up, as usual, and did a great job of it. There was a haze over on the mainland shore, so the sun looked like a big moon rising, complete with an array of orange colors. We took the puppy for her first walk on the beach. There is a strong surf pounding the beach this morning, perfect for boogie boards. It was a little overwhelming for Peligrosa. She kept backing up and whining. The water is just a perfect temperature for swimming right now, but the surf will ring your bell if you're not careful. As usual Diane slept through all this. We had Nacho over for dinner last night and he brought the new chef from Al's backstreet bar. She is a very talented woman. We ate there the night before last, and it was just about the best meal we've had here. She actually knows how to cook fish so that it isn't dried out, and her seasonings are perfect. She also fixed the finest breaded shrimp that I've ever tasted. She speaks only a little English, but we had fun practicing our Spanish and guessing what each other was trying to say. I tried to compliment her in Spanish. Later Nacho told me that the literal translation of what I said was, "Your face looks like dog turds. " It's a good thing that she has a sense of humor or a hearing problem.

It's going to be another busy day here. This weekend we have to go to Ensenada to play a golf tournament. The golf course people here are paying all the expenses for us to represent them. Will have to spend the rest of the week practicing. No not golf, partying. Any fool can play golf, but to truly enjoy some of the fine wines they produce around Ensenada and the good food, is an art form. Unless you've tried it you have no idea how difficult it is to balance the enjoyment of the good life and gluttony, especially when it's free. We'll have to take winter clothes though. It only reaches about 80 degrees over there on the Pacific side and it's downright cold in the mornings. The training schedule today consists of playing nine holes with the La Ventana Golf and Screwdriver Team. I am taking a cooler with the ingredients for screwdrivers so that we don't have to wait until we get to the clubhouse. Of course we will continue the training when we do make it back. We'll have our regular staff meeting, which will include topics ranging from health care (prostrate) nutrition (more orange juice), quantum physics (what is it?) and an open discussion of world and local affairs. We're all too old for affairs, but we still like talking about them. They grow and become more colorful with age. Some of the staff is even beginning to believe their own stories. Remembering is a wonderful thing, if you can only fool yourself into believing yourself.

Will keep you posted as life unfolds here in our sleepy little drinking village with the fishing problem.

# Old People

It seems typical of old people that they spend a lot of time reminiscing about their lives, what could have been, and what they remember of what was. Thirty years ago our company partnered with another local company to build the Tacoma Domed stadium. The other company was owned by Jimmy Zarelli. At that time he was in his 70's, and still worked 6 or 7 days a week, 12 hours a day. He owned several restaurants, a couple of hotels, a good sized construction company, etc. He was reputed to be the richest man in Tacoma. As a result of this project, I went to his office once a week to review construction issues. That would take just a few minutes, then Jimmy would start bumming cigarettes from me and talking about his life. It was absolutely fascinating. He wasn't bragging, just telling stories. He had started as a shoeshine boy, and built his fortune from there. He knew how many meals each of his restaurants served the day before, how many rolls of toilet paper they had used, and of course the profit from each. His brain was amazing. He had all the details of his complex holdings in his head. He also owned the local AAA baseball team. When they were in town, he went to every game. He had the stamina of a teenager. I never tired of listening to him tell about his life, and he was one of the most centered, happy men I have ever known. Making money was his life, and it was pure joy for him. He was good to his people, but knew every move they made, every detail of their jobs. He was also quite frugal. When we were having our meetings, he had just completed a new house for his wife. Not a mansion, just a house. He told me that she wanted a screen for the bathroom window, but he was delaying it to keep her focused on it. He said that as soon as I get her a screen, she'll want something else, like a microwave oven. Jimmy's gone now, but he was a special part of my life for just a little while.

When I was younger, I remember being so impatient with those old people who moved so slow, talked too long, and never wanted to try new things, because they had already figured out that it wouldn't work. In hindsight they were usually right, but a young buck like me was too impatient to really listen. I guess it's part of growing up that we learn to listen and appreciate the richness in other people's lives. This is a good day to learn more about a friend and be impressed with their journey. Try it. You'll love it.

# Things That Make Me Wonder

The circumference of the earth is approximately 25,000 miles. A pulse of light can travel this distance in a little over a second.

At night some of the stars we see are hundreds of light years away. That means the light we are seeing was emitted before we were born.

Viewed in these terms, our world is hardly a freckle on the face of the universe.

As small as it is, our earth is way too large for a person to explore it in an entire lifetime. There are parts of this earth that have never been explored. We are surrounded by a vastness that is beyond our comprehension, and tiny details that cannot be seen with the naked eye. The contrasts can entertain us for hours. For example, we have built huge cities with millions of people. We have damaged a fragile environment, but the natural world has proved to be remarkably durable. Within these cities wildlife survives, and often prospers.

While we have been preoccupied with building empires and single family homes, buying cars, clothes, toys and creating monstrous debts, the birds fly, eat and live just for the moment. They seem to do just fine, and they don't have Zanex to help them through the day.

# Puppy Training – Part II

What a misnomer! Puppy training my ear! Ha!! It's people training. When the puppy peeps, we jump up and take her out to play. When she whines, we leap up and fix her a fresh meal. When she wants to play we drop everything and play with her. This is one very spoiled dog. A typical conversation at our house now is:

"Isn't she cute? Look how she is playing with your toes. Yes, those puppy teeth are sharp, but stop complaining, the bleeding will stop in a few minutes".

We hover over her trying to protect her. She could probably be in Ripley's Believe it or Not as the world's clumsiest dog. She runs into walls, coffee tables, and chairs. Yesterday she fell into the pool again and almost drowned before I got to her. If she had, I would have drowned myself rather than face my wife. On the beach she got sucked up in the surf and we almost lost her there. In the meantime she is busy attacking the other two Chihuahuas who live here. She tries to bite them and usually misses. They nudge her and she falls down and starts all over again. She's a clumsy, slow learner, but can do all these things because she is so cute. Even the other dogs are tolerant of her, except Peso. She sits on top of the couch surveying her kingdom and looking down with distain at her subjects. (That would be us humans who are groveling around on the floor.)

Enough about dogs. I have embarked on a new physical fitness program. Going to the gym has fallen by the wayside. It was too much work to drive over there. OK it was just too boring. Michael told me that if you swim 50 laps a day you would live longer. Well, from my midlife jogging phase 20 years ago, I learned the danger of over training. So now the new program is two laps a day for 25 days. The pool is 40 feet long, so that's 80 feet per day. In just 14 more days I will have done the 50 laps, so will live longer with no stress injuries. Being fit is an important of survival in a third world country. The people here continue to amaze and confound me.

A good example of amazing happened just this week. Tuesday the neighbors were doing past life regressions. We were sitting on the deck when they came out. One woman was weeping. She'd had a vision of herself as a cabin boy with hands bound and being forced to walk the plank. Another woman saw herself as a young man in moccasins running around in the jungle on some sort of male initiation rite. I saw myself wondering what do they put in the water here that does these things to people. But, who am I to judge? Our golf and screwdriver team just spent a young fortune having shirts made up with our logo of crossed golf club and swizzle sticks, and the topics of our staff meeting range from the sublime to the ridiculous. At the last meeting we decided that skinny dipping should be outlawed for anyone over 30. We have formed a committee to examine body types, sizes and shapes to determine who is appropriate to swim naked. At some future date, we will share our observations with the world.

Keep cool, work as little as possible, and love as much as possible.

# San Felipe Morning

Note: I wrote this about four years ago, so nothing of interest is happening in my life right now.

I awoke early this morning, not an unusual occurrence. It's been a very special one. The ocean was in full concert. The surf was bigger than I've ever seen. Big rollers were coming in and curling with white frosting as they attacked the beach. There was the hissing sound of the curls and the pounding providing the bass line to a primitive melody.

The sun strolled into town like a gunfighter from an old western movie. You could feel his cockiness as he climbed up for a better view of his territory. He knows that by midday he will have the townspeople hiding, and moving very slowly if they do attempt to face him. The cosmic inhabitants are trying to put up a defense by hanging a thin layer of clouds on the horizon. That only delays the inevitable. Clouds don't have the strength or determination of a Baja sun.

A crew of workers started work in the courtyard at 5:00AM this morning, putting palm fronds on the palapa they are building. Guess they're trying to beat the sun. They have no chance. Within hours it will be hot, sweaty work. That's the kind that is best delegated. Actually, when you think about it, just about all work is best when delegated. I have a friend who taught me to delegate and disappear.

Lest you think I am wasting my time, I do have a plan for the day. After going to a Sunday brunch with friends and a siesta, I will be working on an inspirational song. The theme is healthy living. The title is "Caffeine, Nicotine, and Tecate Rojo Beer". Would appreciate any input on material for both the chorus and verses. (Have you ever noticed that the spelling for caffeine has the "e" before the "i"? That's odd).

My life is about to change. I've agreed to go to Cabo about the first of August to build a parking lot and mini-storage facility. I went down there a couple of weeks ago to look over the property.

I met with our employee there and he gave me a tour of the town. It's beautiful. It happened to be full of hard bodies in bikinis just out of school. It was also full of nice shops. I told him I should bring my wife down to see all this. He asked me why I would want to bring a sandwich to a banquet. Good point. Initially, I'll be living in a nice trailer next to a freeway overpass. I invited Diane to move down with me and she declined. She said that she is not about to live in a trailer, under a bridge. Another good point.

As Mississippi Steve would say, keep it between the mailboxes and the shiny side up.

# Cashing a Check

I know, your first reaction to this title is, "How could that possible be interesting?"

Well, maybe if I explain that this story is set in a Bancomer office, you will begin to have a glimmer that this just might be worth reading. Anyone who has an account there has stories to tell that confounds all bounds of rational thought or reason. For example, several years ago I applied for a debit card. It took them over a year to issue it, and when they did in had a 0 spending limit. They couldn't change the limit, so had to start the process all over again and issue another card. But that has nothing to do with this story, so why is it included? Who knows, it just popped out of my head. There are several other "pops", but if we start listing them, I'll just be mad all over again.

So, let's try to get back to the story of going to the bank to cash a check. After a few futile tries with their ATM and find them out of money, or accidentally eating my card, we just started going to the bank once a month and cashing a check. Simple, right? Weeelll, maybe not. First if you want to restock the account you have to write a check on your US account. To do that you have to attract the attention of a bank officer and have them initial the check. By the way, this has to be done before noon or they won't accept it. That's not too tough except when the manager is on vacation. During that time they cannot accept checks for deposit. Once you have the initials, and spend your time waiting in line they accept your check, most of the time, and it will clear your bank the following day. However Bancomer won't credit your account until two weeks later.

Enough of this meandering around. Let's go right to the point, however vague it might turn out to be. (It's fun writing this stuff, because I don't know where it's going to end up either.) Yesterday I made the pilgrimage to the bank and it started uneventfully. The nice officer initialed the check, then I went to stand in line. Right in front of me was a small, stocky, young Mexican lady with a big purse. That should have warned me. When it was her turn she plopped the purse on the counter at the window and started pulling out piles of bills. That's ok, because they don't take too long to count. Then she started pulling out plastic bags full of coins. I knew then that it would be a long day.

Finally they sorted all the money and it was my turn. I dashed to the window, eager as a puppy at feeding time. I handed the teller the check to deposit and the one to cash, my driver's license and an affidavit from my first born child. She reached for the checks and spilled two bags of coins all over the floor. That took about 5 minutes while she crawled around on the floor and carefully putting them back in sacks. That done, it can't be long now can it? Ha!! We're just beginning the process. By the way even though your name and account number is printed on the checks, you have to put that plus your address and phone number on the back. So anyway, she starts the processing process. She runs the check through a scanning machine that automatically brings up the information on her computer screen. The then manually inputs all of the same information into the computer, then stares at the screen for a while, so it can catch up. Once the computer is happy, she takes two copies of receipt and MANUALLY PUTS A PIECE OF CARBON PAPER BETWEEN THEM, inserts them in another machine which prints the receipt. She then hands that to you for you to print your name, address, and phone number on that. We're almost there. Now all that is left is for her to give me money. I forgot to mention that it was right after the bank opened that all this is happening. She opens the cash drawer, then realizes that she forgot to stock the drawer, so she leaves her station and heads back into the vault for some cash. That took several minutes. On the way back to her window, she walked by a ringing phone, so she stopped to answer it, and had a nice conversation with someone. At long last she returns and carefully counts out my money and slips it through the window. I feel like I had just run a marathon.

This whole process took a little over half an hour. There was a day several years ago when my reaction would be anger and stress. Actually, the tellers are friendly, they work hard, and are doing the best they can with an archaic system. My only reaction now is to watch the whole show with tolerance and amusement. It was actually an enjoyable and fun experience.

I have to dash off now and start the process to renew my FM2, or whatever they are calling it now with the new immigration laws, that no one understands yet. This should be a lot of fun.

# *Wonder*

Being alive is fascinating beyond words. This morning I was looking out over the Sea of Cortez and drinking coffee. Yum. My mind began to wander, which is not unusual. Random, unconnected, disjointed musings are a daily part of my life. Today the wanderings started at the stars. The light that we see left most of them before any of us were born. That was a long time ago. Scientists tell us that our universe is not infinite, but to my mind, the distances are so huge that it might as well be. Then there is gravity. How does that work? We live on a globe, spinning around the sun. It's kind of melancholy to think that some day the sun will burn out and our earth will wobble around and fall apart. In the meantime there is a moon that circles us, and using the gravity thingy makes the tides that raise and lower the level of the oceans. Why doesn't it seem to do that to lakes? Then I see the pelicans, seagulls, osprey and a host of other birds, whose names I don't have a clue about. What poetry! Their colors, shapes, flight can only be viewed as beautiful. Then there are the changing colors of the water, the blue skies, white clouds, buildings, beaches, people. The complexity of this strains the imagination, and to make it worse (or better, depending on your point of view) this is only a tiny part of the whole picture. There are mountains, trees, plants of infinite varieties, animals not yet seen and prime rib dinners.

There are storms that destroy and even kill. There is sun and rain that heal and rebuild. This duality extends to humans. There are mean vicious people who destroy everything around them, and there are kind loving people who make the world better for all of us. There are governments the same way, and religions too. All of these things are sometimes good, sometimes bad. Our world is too complex to begin to grasp. On one hand we live in an extremely fragile environment, on the other hand the environment can be very flexible and durable. So it seems that no matter what we believe and hold sacred, has an opposite view that is equally valid.

So here we are in the middle of all these contradictions, stumbling along through a life that we can't understand. Aha! Here comes the sermon. The one constant in all this turmoil is that we have choices. They are what really defines who we are and what is the purpose in our lives. We can choose to be bitter, defeated, victims, or, better yet, we can choose to live in joy. We can accept others as they are, seeing the God in each of them. We can focus on the beauty of our natural world. We can believe that good comes from every bad. As I write this it's New Year's eve. We are facing January, the coldest, darkest month of the year. But it thrills me to know that in this low, are the seeds of spring. The sun has started moving North for the summer. The days are becoming longer, however slowly, and soon spring will be here. That is a parallel to life. In the darkest of times the seeds of a brighter future are planted. So, dear friends, go plant seeds and enjoy waiting and watching them to grow into a better life.

# Strange Weather

- Summertime 2009

Strange weather. For the last week its been cloudy, windy, and cooler than normal. I heard that its been hot in the Northwest lately. My theory is that the heat is being sucked out of the Baja, leaving us with 80-90 degree weather. That's a treat this time of year. The clouds are unusual too. Obviously they have become homeless since they left the Northwest, so they drifted south, not unlike a lot of our compadres down here. Yesterday we had clouds all over the sky, and they almost looked like they wanted to rain. Of course they burned off, and left us panting once again. Its like an adolescent trying to pubertize. They keep trying to rain, but haven't figured out how yet.

We're looking forward to today. Paco and I have been trying to learn to sing together. Its improving but way too slowly, so we invited some of the local musicians over to our courtyard this afternoon. We're going to swim, drink beer, and take a singing lesson. It will probably be like trying to teach a pig to sing. Frustrating for the teacher, and irritating for the pig. Well its at least an excuse to party. We've been working on "Blue Eyes Cryin' in the Rain" for a month now. It's still not quite ready to go on tour.

Five years ago when we first came here, there were no gringos here in the summer. This year there are hundreds of us. We went to a brand new steak house last night with a few friends. 20 people showed up. The woman sitting on the other side of me (Of course Diane was on one side of me) had big boobs and a low cut dress. I'll find out if Diane is speaking to me when she wakes up. Do you have any idea how difficult it is to act casual, stare, watch your wife, and talk all at the same time? That is STRESS.

Our golf tournament scheduled for late October is sold out, and we have recruited 4 different car dealerships to have cars as prizes for hole in ones. I have never heard of that before. Usually you may get one car on one of the holes. Another man, who has a Panama hat company is sponsoring us for several thousand and donating some expensive hats., Tecate Beer is giving $20,000 cash and free beer all weekend. The list goes on. Now people are trying to get in, so we're selling non-golfing sponsorships for a thousand dollars, just so they can have their names on the program. We will end up raising $150,000 to $175,000 this year. This is just way too much fun.

In the interest of full disclosure, it's not all fun and games here. Paradise is not perfect. There is a bird, probably a very big one, who poops on our breakfast nook window about once a week. It's a second story window, so difficult to reach to clean. Words cannot describe how distressing that is. Well, they probably can but it isn't worth giving you more details. Every morning we arise, not knowing if this is the day it will happen again. I kind of admire the bird. We can't catch him, and he attacks with impunity. All we can do is wash windows. Who says animals aren't smart?

Well, enough for today. Remember that no matter how caring you are, some people are just assholes.

# Thanksgiving Letter

Hola, friends and family. I haven't written in a long time because I didn't have anything to say. Still don't , but decided to write anyway. I hope this doesn't turn out like those family letters that people used to write this time of year. You remember them, the ones that went like:

*Hi everyone. It's been a good year at the Woodcock household. Billy just got paroled and has been clean for almost a week now. He is planning on going to medical school as soon as he gets his GED. Betty Sue, our 12 year old, just had twins. They are sooo cute. One of them looks like he has some oriental blood, but who can tell in this day and age. Edgar and I are thinking about retiring as soon as the trailer is paid for, but aren't sure how that would affect his disability pay. His back still bothers him after the accident at the Roundhouse. (How could he have known that stranger was a professional wrestler). Anyway it's been 11 years since he's been able to work, but the disability keeps us in beer.*

Life here in Mexico still has its slow, wonderful pace. This summer someone took out a bunch of stop signs around town. You may recall that last year they sent a load of them down from Mexicali, so the crew just randomly placed them all over town. Main streets had stop signs, while side roads had none. It was truly baffling. When all the signs came down, it looked like vandalism, but after 3 months none had been replaced. I began to think that maybe common sense and reason had invaded our village. Silly me. Last week a new batch went up. The good news is that the shipment this time didn't have as many signs as last time, so there are still a few intersections that aren't plugged up with women and teenagers (and younger) often ignoring the signs, and old gringos who are terrified to even enter the intersection. We still don't have a traffic light. That's a good thing because the culture here is not too responsive to precise directions. We are a growing community though. Yesterday I saw a truck that was reasonably new and didn't have any flat tires. San Felipe has always been the town where cars and trucks go to die. Seeing a respectable looking one was a watershed day.

It was roughly 2007 when I wrote this. It is fun to reminisce about the old days here. Now we have lots of cars that are in reasonable shape, a supermarket and lots of jobs at the gold mine. As the population ratchets up, we see life moving a little faster, and not nearly as relaxed. Oh well, that's progress, I guess.

# The Weather Report

It's been a cooler than normal summer here in our sleepy little drinking village. There hasn't been a single day where it was too hot to play golf. Yesterday was downright comfortable. It has been windy, which has irritated the sea. There have been whitecaps for the last two weeks, and some serious surf. Our beach has been pure, fine sand for several years at least. All the surf has pulled the sand off the beach and now its rocks and gravel. The surf is now trying to turn the gravel into sand, rolling it back and forth with the tide changes. I doubt that it will be done by Labor day. The ocean is quite warm now, the perfect temperature for swimming, but the surf will beat you to death. We are somehow managing to cope with these hardships.

Had an informal songwriting conference by the swimming pool last week. We swam, drank beer, then critiqued each others songs. My guitar fingers were sore from all that mashing on the wires by the time we quit. My favorite song of the day has a great melody line, fun chord sequence and good lyrics. It's called "I'm a Weed in the Garden of Love, and I Just got Plucked". Next time we get together I'll play it for you. It's a very sentimental love song. (well, sort of).

Living in a third world country, you learn to adjust your expectations. A fine restaurant here is one with a window air conditioner that sort of works. A gourmet meal is one served on a real plate, and not wrapped in a tortilla. Presentation and taste are not considered important. Driving is a sport, not an art and things like turn indicators, headlights and windshields are optional accessories not found on a lot of cars. These standards apply to music here too. I have been offered several gigs, including being piano player for a new group. (We now have a piano tuner in town, so at least the few pianos here don't sound quite as awful as they did). I've also been invited to play guitar at a couple of places in town. (You would probably think them disreputable, but again, for here they're upscale.) As you age, you gain a little bit of wisdom (ok, not always) and I like to think that's happened to me. Not being a big fan of public humiliation, I have not even been tempted to accept the offers. By the way, none of them offered to pay me, which is a key economic indicator of my value as a musician.

I'm planning a trip to the Northwest mid August, and look forward to seeing all of you, or at least the decent parts of you. I hope you enjoy reading this dribble. If you are on my list, and would rather not, please let me know. I don't want to be a pest.

Please send this to 5 other people, and something good might happen to you.

If not, tough.

# It's January

My how time flies. It seems like just yesterday that it was
October. That was a wonderful month with warm weather and lots
of sun. Living here on the Baja we know that a day without
sunshine is night. (Note to self: You're supposed to be writing
about January. Pay attention you fool!) Oh, Yes. Well anyway,
it's January and cold, sort of. All over town people are whining
and sniveling about how miserable they are, freezing to death and
can hardly wait for it to warm up. These same people will
complain that it is too hot when that happens. It's a shame how we
often take our blessings for granted. The little town of Foul
Habits North Dakota is was 30 below at noon yesterday. Snow
was piled up so high that it would reach a giraffe's ass, had there
been any giraffes there. If you were crazy enough to try to pee
outdoors, it would freeze before it hit the ground. Here we can do
that year round. And here we are complaining that it was only 60
degrees today. Most of us are fortunate enough to have warm
clothes, a house to keep us cozy and hot buttered rum. We should
be celebrating our good fortune, like some of the tourists from up
North. You can see them around town, and out on the golf course
wearing tee shirts and shorts. We, in the meantime are wearing
long underwear, sweatshirts, jackets and ski hats. We've had the
heat on in our house for as much as 3 or 4 hours at a time, but most
of the time it really isn't necessary.

Isn't it fascinating that we humans can find something to complain
about in just about any situation. Reminds me of the old cliché
"He'd complain if he was hung with a new rope". (Another note:
That is grammatically incorrect. That is a subjunctive case so it
should be "were" instead of "was"). Oh well, you get the point.
The people who light up our lives are those rare individuals who
see the positive in any situation. They find joy in a cold day
because they are alive. They see a spilled drink as an opportunity
to pour another one. They see a blown engine in their car as an
opportunity to buy a brand new one. You know someone who fits
this bill. Why don't we try an experiment and find something
happy about everything we do today? If enough people do this, it
could just change the world. My sister told me years ago that we

should try to see the God in the people around us. Try doing that while you're standing in line at the bank, or at the immigration office. It really works for me, and hopefully will work for you and make your life better.

Well I better sign off. I have no idea how what started as a discussion of January weather turned into a sermon on how to live your life. Now it's time for me to shower and go change the light bulbs at the pro shop. We are converting it to an art gallery with only art that is made in Mexico. So we need to replace lights that have been burned out for years to brighten the place. Let's all go out and bring new light to today.

# Wimmin

To state the obvious, men and women are different. I have been thinking about writing this for about a month now. One trait that characterizes men is their penchant for doing foolish things. Just look at those extreme sports shows on TV with men jumping out of airplanes without parachutes, driving all kinds of ill suited vehicles over cliffs, or into walls, you know what I mean. For a married man, like me, to write about women falls into that same class. It is foolish, even suicidial. A recently divorced man told me that there are three rings involved in a marriage. There is the engagement ring, the wedding ring and suffe-ring. But it isn't my intent to bash marriage. What follows is an objective, rational, carefully reasoned examination and explanation of what makes women tick. Hopefully, living in Mexico, I can do this without being sued by some rabid man hater.

Twenty years ago some fool with a doctorate degree in some arcane science tried to explain the difference by studying the brains of men and women. He concluded that thought processing involves both sides of the brain and women have multiple cross connections, just like a freeway. Men, on the other hand, have a single path, which he compared to a donkey trail. As a result, my wife has been calling me "donkey brain" for twenty years. You may have thought that elephants have long memories. HA! The number of grudges and the number of years they can hold onto them is staggering. Not even a huge supercomputer can compete with that capacity.

Comparatively, men are quite simple. We do think about more than beer and sex. We also think about expensive toys, you know, race cars, boats, planes, fishing gear, golf clubs. So at a cocktail party men separate from the women and talk about just that. Toys, beer, and finally sex. We've all had that conversation on the way home when the wife asks, "What did you guys talk about tonight?" One sentence is all it takes to answer. (If we're thinking straight, we omit any reference to sex). She will then probe for details. We don't remember any. The only defense for this grilling is to ask what she talked to her girlfriends about. That is good for at least 30 minutes of incredibly detailed accounting of the entire evening. It will also include a description of what they all wore, and hairstyles. The danger here is that may lead to the question, "Did you see that outfit on Evelyn?" The correct answer is no, even if you do remember. If you answer yes you will be required to critique it. At best, all you probably remember is the cleavage. That too, would be a big mistake to admit.

Well, maybe that scientist had a point. What a woman remembers, especially our mistakes, is a huge volume of detailed information that never fades. Us males just don't have the capacity for all that data, nor do we have the inclination to care. We do remember successful fishing trips and essential sports facts, but beyond that things get pretty hazy. I guess the most important piece of advice here is just to remember the phrase, "yes dear".

# Yummy

Last night was a helluva a night at our house. At about 5:00PM Nacho, Tony, and Lily showed up at our door, loaded with utensils and food. Where do I start to describe the perfect evening? How about we do some introductions first.

Nacho – Well actually he is Ignacio, but no one uses that name for him. He is the head greenskeeper at the golf course and in a previous life played the Mexican pro golf tour. He is a good and kind man and very competent at what he does. More to the point, he is an amazing chef. His barbequed ribs are the best you'll ever taste, and he does a wide range of Mexican cooking, each dish being in the gourmet class. We have never had food of any kind as good as what he cooks. His tacos gobernador just melt in your mouth. For the uninitiated it's a shrimp taco with secret ingredients. This list could go on ad nauseum. What he doesn't know about tequila isn't worth knowing. He sips it, then sucks on an orange, not the traditional lime. The orange is the perfect complement to the tequila and makes it taste much better. Try it. Guaranteed, or your money back.

Tony – Actually Antonio, but no one uses that either, he's just Tony. He's Nacho's assistant and he drives the crews. He is perfect for the job. He had a difficult period earlier in his life. He is covered with gang tattoos and is big, strong and can intimidate the crap out of strong men. Since he arrived on the scene, the golf course crews are always working, and seldom seen just standing around. However, Tony is the kindest, nicest man you'll ever meet, and fiercely loyal to his friends. The only thing of value he brought to the party, aside from being delightful company, was Lily.

Lily – She is Tony's other half, and a great cook in her own right. We all still remember one night when Nacho came over to cook chiles relleno. Nacho got a little carried away with the testing of tequila brands, and was temporarily incapacitated. Lily saved the day by cooking them herself, and they were excellent. But that's another story. Anyway, Lily had made fresh dough that afternoon for tortillas. She shaped the dough and rolled them out while

Nacho was cooking the chiles verde. Tortillas are a mainstay of any diet down here, and good ones are all over town, but Lily's were the most tender, moist perfect ones we'd ever tasted. They alone could have made a good meal.

OK. Now to the good part. It was one of those nights when everyone was in a good mood. Good conversation flowed effortlessly, switching from Spanish to English and back continually. While we had cocktails and conversation, Nacho and Lily cooked. Incidentally, they managed to have a drink while they were cooking, so they weren't totally left out. Nacho is an efficient cook. He moves fast, chopping dicing, frying, boiling things al at the same time. He prepared some frijoles (beans) of course. Can't have a Mexican meal without them. He carefully trimmed green onions, and cut radishes in fancy shapes to give a touch of class to the plates. The crowning achievement was the chiles verde. They were heavenly. They were fantastic. They were unbelievably good. They were orgasmic. With Nacho it's difficult to find out everything he puts in a recipe. He did teach me how to make the best guacamole in town about a year ago. Anyway, last night it was little squares of pork, browned then boiled in a green sauce that included cilantro, green peppers, poblano peppers, and some basic salsa ingredients that he put in the blender then cooked the whole thing for a couple of hours on a very low heat. That mixture is then wrapped in Lily's tortillas and topped with sour cream. It was one of the best meals of my life. So we gorged ourselves and sort of collapsed in the living room for a few minutes. They then did the dishes, cleaned the kitchen, said goodnight and left. They put the friend in friendship. Generous, kind, talented wonderful people. Our little village is blessed to have so many people like them. It is indeed the good life.

# Windy

Yesterday was windy. Very windy. With the wind comes the dust from the desert that surrounds our little village. As it picks up energy, the dust obscures the sun and turns the day into a brown, drab event. The dust is so fine that it penetrates hermetically sealed containers, and leaves a layer of dirt throughout our leaky casas. That's good news for people in the housecleaning business, but irritating to the rest of us. We need rain. It has been more months than I can count since we had any rain. It has been in the forecast a couple of times, but when it comes time to perform, the clouds dissipate and leave us dry. When it does rain, it puts a little crust on the desert sand, and keeps the dirt in place when it blows. After months of no rain, the crust is worn off and we start having these dust storms that can pile several feet of sand across the highway and turn our world brown. The only problem with that is that even a half inch of rain will flood the downtown area. Under a thin layer of sand, the ground here is  hard and impervious to water, so anything that falls immediately runs off. The town is next to the Sea of Cortez so it's at the low point, and all that water runs right onto the main street. Shops are flooded. Stock is damaged, and it usually takes a few days for the water to be pumped out. In the meantime, we have to shop at the places that are on higher ground. All of the good bars are in the low areas, so it creates a crisis for some of our more outgoing neighbors.

Today there were no horizon clouds to add color to the sunrise, so it was pretty plain, almost like it bad a hangover from yesterday. The wind is still blowing so offroad dune buggy trips or golf are not on today's agenda. In my case, out of desperation for something to do, I may actually go to the office and do some work. Just saying that word makes me shudder. Such is life in a third world country. It is so rare when the weather here is not ideal, that we're not equipped to adjust to these semi-harsh conditions. Suggestions for coping with this stress will be gladly accepted, reviewed with great interest, added to our New Year's resolutions, and promptly forgotten, because the weather will be back to normal by then.

We do have something to look forward to tonight. We're having our office Christmas party. OK it's a little late, but time slips away and planning ahead is not something we do much of here. We're having a gourmet dinner and have hand made coffee cups for everyone. They were made locally in a kiln that we moved down here from the States. They are really beautiful, and each one is different. It's fun to have something from San Felipe, made by one of our customers. We have two and a half employees. When you add close relatives that brings the total for the dinner to 20 people. I will be giving the welcome speech in Spanish, so it is highly unlikely that anyone will have a clue what I'm trying to say. The good news is that it will be really short due in part, at least, to my very limited vocabulary.

Laugh at something today. You'll feel better.

Made in the USA
San Bernardino, CA
10 April 2014